Using his personal commi
servant leadership practice in
this commitment to leadership
poor and disadvantaged with renewed passion. Dave researched
various biblical and other sources, presenting why compassion for
the poor is often no longer a central commitment of the Western
Church today, and then suggests how the church's meaningful
participation in this priority enterprise will support Jesus special
concern for the poor and, in turn, attract people to a day-to-
day life of compassion and service. The book is a 'must read'
for those wanting to revitalize their own individual life or with
others in the institutional church. It is an encouraging book that
stirs readers to a shared church vision that energizes and guides
decision-making towards collective follow-through action for the
poor at home or elsewhere.

Dr. Stan Remple
Director of the M.A. in Leadership, Trinity Western University

Speaking to our hearts and our heads, this challenges us to
stop turning a blind eye and calls us to action. Straight forward
and clear as day; we know that the church needs a major re-boot
in order to face the future and Dave has given us that picture in
terms of our worldwide impact. If we want to remain alive, this is
one of the things that the Western Church must address. We have
built an organization, called "the church", which is repulsing the
next generation. Their hearts cry for justice in our dealings with
the rest of the world. Dave calls the Church to change, to action,
and to justice.

Rev. David Brotherton, MA
National Youth Director, Christian & Missionary Alliance in Canada
Associate Professor of Youth Ministry, Ambrose University College

Rooted in excellent biblical, social and cultural research this is a prophetic call to the western Church to live out Jesus' kingdom mission to the least, the hurting, and the forgotten. It's a call for every one of us who call ourselves followers of Jesus Christ to die to ourselves so that we (and others) can have life!

Rev. Dr. Ric D. Strangway
Lead Pastor, North Point Community Church

The book presents a clear reflection of our culture. This is an authentic critique of our selfish society, which is dominated by self-seekers, hypocrites, sadists and lavish property mongers. Dave stresses the discernable public sentiment that the few are unjustly profiting in excess at the expense of the majority in the world. This is an awakening call to all of us who have remained blind to our evil ways. The poor who are the majority are experiencing discrimination. This is a call to all who are able to take the example of Jesus seriously. "Wherever your treasure is, there the desires of your heart will also be." Matthew 6: 19-21

H. E. Ambassador Simon Nabukwesi
Kenyan High Commissioner, Canada

Hungry For Life

A Vision of the Church that
Would Transform the World

DAVE BLUNDELL

WestBow
PRESS

WestBow Press™
A Division of Thomas Nelson
1663 Liberty Drive
Bloomington, IN 47403
www.westbowpress.com
Phone: 1-866-928-1240

Cover Design and Photography by: Ryan Toyota and Ginnie Frede

First published by WestBow Press: 02/05/2010

ISBN: 978-1-4497-0022-5 (e)
ISBN: 978-1-4497-0023-2 (sc)
ISBN: 978-1-4497-0024-9 (hc)

Library of Congress Control Number: 2010920673

Printed in the United States of America
Bloomington, Indiana

This book is printed on acid-free paper.

Dedication

To my three best friends and partners in transformation:

Heidi, Caleb, and Abby.

Contents

Acknowledgements

None of these thoughts are originally mine. No one ever has completely independent thoughts. These thoughts have been formed by Scripture, for all truth is originally His.

Heidi, Caleb, and Abby have empowered and encouraged me to live this ideal and dream. Without their above and beyond commitment and sacrifice God would have chosen someone else to do what we do. The freedom to go into the world with those three partners standing behind me is simply indescribable. My greatest fear is to leave this world to my children the way it was given to me. Also, it was my Mom who taught and modeled compassionate, selfless empathy, and my Dad from whose lips I first heard that the priorities of today's Church seemed far from Christ's.

Our work has been formed by some great books that have taught me about poverty, worship, the Church, leadership, and what the Scriptures teach on these topics. Many of these authors have unknowingly been my mentors. Many of them I have quoted.

The practical daily application of these scriptural ideas has been driven into my soul by dozens of incredible people who live in developing nations, many of whom I refer to in this book. These great people have unknowingly taught me that they have far more to give us in the West than we can ever give them. It has been through their physical poverty that my spiritual poverty has become acutely apparent. Through their suffering they know Jesus like I don't.

The staff and board at Hungry For Life have been my partners in helping me process these ideas for years. Although Hungry For Life is relatively new, many of the relationships are not. It's been through these relationships that God has molded my heart and mind. Anything of value that has been accomplished through Hungry For Life reflects the work of this amazing team. They are simply fun to serve with.

To those who support us with their prayers and finances, as I have said many times, without you doing what you are doing, we simply can't do what we are doing.

I also want to thank my editorial team: Heidi Blundell, Ken Schamuhn, Kristine den Boon, Annalise Schamuhn, Julie Beukema and Charlene Stinson. You all made me sound so much better than I really am.

Finally, why God chose me to be His and chose me to do this is beyond me. And He has proven to me time and time again that there is nothing of any eternal value that I could ever produce on my own.

Amos 5 – All Show, No Substance

(Excerpts from The Message)

[10-12]People hate this kind of talk.
Raw truth is never popular.
But here it is, bluntly spoken:
Because you run roughshod over the poor
and take the bread right out of their mouths,
You're never going to move into the
luxury homes you have built.
You're never going to drink wine from the
expensive vineyards you've planted.
[14]Seek good and not evil— and live!
You talk about God...being your best friend.
Well, live like it, and maybe it will happen.
[15]Hate evil and love good, then work it out in the public square.
Maybe God...will notice your remnant and be gracious.
[21-24]"I can't stand your religious meetings.
I'm fed up with your conferences and conventions.
I want nothing to do with your religion projects,
your pretentious slogans and goals.
I'm sick of your fund-raising schemes,
your public relations and image making.
I've had all I can take of your noisy ego-music.
When was the last time you sang to me?
Do you know what I want?
I want justice—oceans of it.
I want fairness—rivers of it.
That's what I want. That's all I want."

Foreword

Dave has given empirical data to persuade readers to reassess themselves with regard to the contribution they are making to improve human relations and the well-being of the poor in the world. The author strikes me as an embodiment of a superb creative thinker, a determined researcher, and a role model Christian leader with obvious moral strength, guided by a dedicated spirit to do good in society, especially among the poor. He is a writer from the school of realism; he demonstrates this with examples as experienced during his visits to various communities in the world, or as narrated by his partners and colleagues.

His narratives point to major tragedies that kill approximately 10 million children under the age of 5 year after year (approximately 27,000 per day), many due to hunger and easily preventable causes. This goes unnoticed because, "Some tragedies have no smoke or flame to describe the intensity" (Professor Khawaja Mahboob). Dave takes us through reflections on our lives and relationships, giving examples that we live in a swirling tide of events, dreams, promises, situations, threats, opportunities and challenges.

Dave gives a critical assessment of the conflicts in the world. He seems to advance the theory that civilization does not drop from the sky; it has always been the result of good leadership under enlightened, passionate and caring leaders who influence others with their ideas and by the example of their lives. He brings out the idea that the strong must show humility and kindness to the weak by sharing what they have.

The writer has conducted good research supporting a strong conviction that the uses of military force alone will never bring peace in the world. He argues that passion, empathy and humanitarian assistance will win the hearts of recipients. Thus culminating in a new perception about human life: as long as children and the poor are allowed to die preventable deaths, then there are very few true Christians exhibiting true love in this world. He concludes that goodness, thoughtfulness and faith in God's own example are the only investments that will not fail human beings. By this, he has challenged church leaders and Christians in the developed world to renew their spirituality.

The book presents a clear reflection of our culture. This is an authentic critique of our selfish society, which is dominated by self-seekers, hypocrites, sadists and lavish property mongers. Dave stresses the discernable public sentiment that the few are unjustly profiting in excess at the expense of the majority in the world. This is an awakening call to all of us who have remained blind to our evil ways. The poor who are the majority are experiencing discrimination. Dave seems to agree with Mother Teresa who is quoted to have said, "The biggest disease in the world today is not leprosy or tuberculosis, but rather the feeling of being unwanted."

This is a call to all who are able to take the example of Jesus seriously. "Wherever your treasure is, there the desires of your heart will also be" (Matthew 6:19-21).

H.E. Ambassador Simon Nabukwesi
Kenya High Commissioner, Canada

INTRODUCTION - Status Quo is Not an Option

The Role of Corporate Vision in Change

Both the status quo of the state of the Western Church and the suffering in the developing world are simply unacceptable and godlessly starved for life. This reality can easily leave those that are concerned feeling despondent. Almost daily, the bad news of a broken world points toward a solid hope that somewhere there must be good news on the horizon. The precedent of history tells us that the worse a situation is the closer we are to the essential environment for transformation. The darker the night, the more welcome the dawn.

Knowing there is something inherently immoral and absolutely wrong with the degree of suffering in this world of abundance, it is natural for people to at least hope for some sort of transformation or a solution to the problem. That hope of change can also lead most to at least question their personal role in the issues and in a proposed solution. However, people need to be able to look to leaders who can confidently paint the picture of a preferred future and point in the direction of that new reality.

In the fall of 2006, I asked our staff and board the most critical question of our organization's existence, past and future. We engaged in a year-long discussion to answer the question, "If Hungry For Life had only 50 years to exist, if we knew we only had until 2056, what would we want the Church and the world to look like because we existed?" I asked the same question in a few different ways. "If we only had 18,250 more days to live, what would we want to see changed in the Church and in the world? What will be our legacy as an organization? If finances weren't an obstacle, to what end would we want to spend our lives? Picture all of us sitting together in our retirement homes commenting on the condition of the Church and the world in 2056. What is happening? How specifically are the Church and the world different today than they were way back in 2006?" The answer to those questions became our shared vision.

Much has been made of the word *vision* within organizational life and leadership theory in the profit and not-for-profit sectors, inside and outside the Church. I would guess that, within most organizations, the process of identifying and articulating a vision results in a vague, nice sounding but detached-from-daily-reality statement that is framed in the office or printed on a brochure. But ask the average staff member, volunteer, supporter, or even board member to succinctly articulate why the organization exists, and to what end, and you might get an awkward description that remotely sounds like something the Executive Director said at the annual retreat last year. Nonetheless, the potential and power of vision is the stuff that alters the course of history.

Vision is a powerful thing in the life of an individual and an organization. My heart pounded when I first read Andy Stanley's description of vision:

> Visions are born in the soul of a man or woman who is consumed with the tension between what is and what could be. Anyone who is emotionally involved – frustrated, brokenhearted, and maybe even angry – about the way things are in light of the way they believe things could be, is a candidate for a vision. Visions form in the hearts of those who are dissatisfied with the status quo.[1]

The first time I remember being motivated to change something was when I was about 10 years old, after my grandma died from cancer. Just a few years prior, my grandpa had died from the same disease. I first watched him get sick and, before I even really understood serious illness or the realities of death, I watched him waste away. Only 6 at the time, I vividly remember the night he passed away. Worse than my own feelings of loss, it was more difficult for me to watch my mom grieve the loss of her dad. Then, just a couple of years after his death, cancer struck my grandma. Again, we watched helplessly as she was consumed by the horrible disease over a two year period. For a second time, only this time even more painfully, I grieved the loss of someone I loved so much. Deeply broken again, I watched the gut wrenching effects of my mom grieving the loss of another parent. Cancer had now orphaned my mom. My sadness then turned to anger. My anger then turned to action. Something had to change and I was going to do something about it.

The first thing I did was set up my microscope (remember I was 10 at the time), determined to find the cure for cancer. I had read about great people like Louis Pasteur, who had found cures and vaccinations for many diseases that plagued people at the time. Motivated by being all too acquainted with the pain of death, losing three of his five children within seven years, as well as watching thousands die of cholera, typhoid, and rabies, his life's mission was to prevent people from experiencing what he had.[2] He brought hope to humanity by preventing the deaths of so many. Like Pasteur, the personal pain I experienced and watched told me something was wrong in the world and, combined with the hope for change, it motivated me to set up my little toy microscope and chemistry set and start looking for the vaccination or cure for cancer. I went out in the backyard and gathered a handful of dirt, leaves, flowers, and probably a dead bug and looked at this stuff under a real toy microscope hoping that one of these specimens would have a tiny label "Cure for Cancer."

Needless to say, it only took me about 20 minutes to realize all I had accomplished was to make a mess in the basement. Yet that wouldn't stop me. Thinking that it was probably best to leave finding cures for diseases to people with more than a grade four education, my Mom told me that I could help them by raising money for the Cancer Society. That was the answer! I could raise buckets of money to find a cure. I organized my little brother to help me hold a car wash in our driveway. This being before printers and computers, and with no access to a photocopier, we wrote out by hand dozens of little flyers telling everyone on our block that we were holding a "Car Wash For Cancer." On the big day I was shocked by how many cars came. My eight year old brother and I washed these cars like mad while people sat on the lawn chairs which were our waiting area. Later in the day a police car pulled into the driveway and I thought, "Oh no! We must be in trouble because we went around the neighborhood putting these flyers underneath people's windshield wipers, and that was probably against the law." Instead the local police heard about the fundraiser and brought over a couple of police cars to be washed. Wow! This was now a big time fundraiser because even the police were involved. At the end of the long and very wet day, we counted all the money we had raised. $70 was the grand total and it might as well have been $7 million to us (probably my parent's water bill for the month was more than the $70 we raised). The next day we rode our bikes down to the local bank, which was collecting money for the Cancer Society, to make our big presentation. I was overwhelmed by the thought that maybe, just maybe, my vision of curing cancer could now be realized with this huge $70 donation. I was consumed by the painful reality of what was, compared to the dream of what could be.

At the age of 10, because it affected us both so deeply, it was fairly easy to convince my little brother to buy into a vision of curing cancer. Years later, however, I came to understand that to make a significant difference globally I needed people - lots of people - to join me; gifted and passionate people who would share the ideal of a different future. The first and most significant role of a servant leader within an organization is to facilitate the process of articulating a shared vision of a preferred future.[3] A vision of "what can be" versus "what is" can be so compelling that it causes people to sacrifice personal comfort and security, to give of their time and treasure, to see purpose in the perceived menial tasks, and to look beyond petty differences, all toward seeing the vision become reality. Vision calls out the best in us: our gifts, our talent, and our commitment to excellence. Leaders who champion vision serve by giving people the ability to get to the end of their lives fully convinced they spent themselves with no regrets. People don't look for a leader who will defend or refine the status quo: they will look for and follow a leader who will paint for them a vision of a new reality leading them out of the status quo and into change. Then they will continue to follow a leader who engages them in the process of change and collective discovery of the new future.

However, casting a vision is only the start. It's dangerous to cast a shared vision and think it will stick or automatically become reality. Inflating the hopes of people by articulating a compelling dream and then not following through with tangible strategy for realizing the dream is more destructive than not casting the vision in the first place. Great leaders live in two worlds: they live with one foot solidly in the world of "what is" and they also live with the other foot solidly in the world of the "not yet." Effective visionary leaders can live in the reality of the present and can also live in the possibility of a different future.[4] Closing the gap between what exists and what *should* exist is where great visionary leaders are separated from dreamers. Effective change agents need to be focused on the immediacy of improving operations, planning strategic growth, and caring for the people they lead, all without taking their eyes off the future vision.

A servant leader must then always look for ways to constantly keep that vision before all of the organization's stakeholders, celebrating the small and large "wins" of the vision becoming a reality. The daily grind can so easily focus people's attention on the immediate that they lose site of the "why" in the vortex of activity. People's imaginations will only be captivated so long before they need to see some evidence of the vision: they need to be inspired to stay motivated to see momentum develop into a movement of effective results.

We are created to exist for something great. We were crafted by and for the image of God which presupposes that there is something within all of us that craves meaning, purpose, and fulfillment. We desire not simply to exist, but to live for something far greater than ourselves.

> Whether we are speaking of the CEO or the shipping clerk, every human being needs to feel that he or she is making some sort of contribution. Great leaders appreciate this hunger and constantly communicate to their followers how what they do in their work positively affects the world at large. To put it simply, these leaders give their followers a reason to get up in the morning.[5]

Sadly, today, the majority of people both inside and outside the Church live a robot existence going through the motions and stages of life, all the while wondering if there is something more than this. As we will see in detail later, there is an ever-growing, dissatisfied group of religious church attendees, myself included, who have seen the discrepancy between what we read about the life of Christ lived out through the New Testament Church and the status quo of an average North American or European Church in this twenty-first century. At the same time, this world is broken and desperately hungry for the real life which we read is readily available for those who follow and emulate Christ.

Hungry For Life exists because we are convinced there is a problem - no, a crisis - that must be addressed. We believe that the Church in the West is spiritually and morally bankrupt and we also believe that it is incomprehensible that about half of the world population suffers from easily preventable causes. We exist to address the problem of spiritual and physical poverty. Yet, we also strongly believe in the reality that God has already provided all of the spiritual and physical resources necessary to affect change that will revive the Church and transform the world.

So, if we are convinced that the world is broken and desperately hungry for life and we are also convinced that God has already provided everything needed to satisfy spiritual and physical hunger, then why is there so much spiritual and physical hunger in the world? If we have the cure for the disease why are so many still spiritually and physically terminal? It's this reality that keeps me up at night. It's this frustration and holy anger that forges within us a resolve for change and forces us into a position of "I can't not do this." It's this place of holy discontent that Bill Hybels refers to when he writes:

> The most inspired, motivated, and driven people I know are the ones who live their lives from the energy of their holy discontent. They have a constant awareness that what is wrecking them is wrecking the heart of God. Refusing to stay fed up, though, they instead get fueled by their restless longing for the better-day realities God

says are coming soon. They listen to the soulish instinct inside them that says life just doesn't have to be the way that most people experience it. Most importantly, they suit up and jump into the game when God says, "If you'll hook up with me, I'll involve you in effecting some much needed change around here!"[6]

It is out of this holy discontent that our staff and board answered that question I asked them in the fall of 2006, and we answered with the following:

We envision a world transformed by a global movement of compassion and justice evidenced by the eradication of needless suffering. A world transformed and characterized by: a passionate, unified Church speaking with a voice of credibility, realized by its reputation for love and compassion, churches and organizations strategically connected and engaged with communities around the world, involved in sustainable community development, and generous living that has resulted in a redistribution of global resources.

A clear personal and corporate vision – the reason we believe that God has placed us on His creation – keeps us focused on the "why." It enables us to withstand external opposition. It emboldens us to overcome real or perceived barriers and impassions us to make sacrifices that test our faith to make room for the demonstration of the power of God. The role of vision within Hungry For Life is also vital because we ask our staff to walk into a life of raising their own support. Our staff must be absolutely convinced that their personal vision aligns with our corporate vision and be able to communicate that message clearly to people who might invest their finances to support our staff's work. As a result, one of the first and most important ways I can serve our staff is to champion our vision.

While vision does serve our organization with inspiration, focus, and resolve, the whole world is desperate for a vision of hope and change. In a world with so much bad news, people want to be inspired by the hope that life can be different. The most recent election in the United States has demonstrated the power that comes from inspiring hope for change. Unfortunately, that hope is still misplaced. While the leaders of our world do have the ability to affect change, either good or bad, these agents are still mortal and their change is temporal. The life for which this world is hungry comes from none other than the Author of Life. The world is desperate for a Church whose effectiveness is commensurate with its claims of power and transformational potential, and it is toward this end that we do everything we do, including writing this book.

Above all, I pray that the results of this book are twofold: people will say they have heard from God a prophetic call to pay attention to Him and to the poor and needy; and that the call will contribute to the transformation of the world. I pray that no longer will the Church in the West be known for its irrelevance, boredom, and hypocrisy. Instead, I pray that the Church will be motivated and mobilized to recover its mission of being a force of love and compassion, pointing the nations to the greatness of the One we claim to follow and represent.

One evening I was helping my then 2 year old son through the bedtime routine. I gave him his bedtime snack, bathed him, helped him brush his few teeth, put on his warm pajamas, tucked him into his warm bed, and lay beside him until he fell asleep. It was one of those "sleeping child" moments that every parent loves to hold onto. However, this wonderfully thankful moment with my son was suddenly trashed by something I had read only days before. At that point in my life I was struggling through my calling, vocation, and personal vision. For years, I wrestled with the big issues of global poverty, injustice, and the fact that the Church of Jesus Christ demonstrates little urgency to do anything about it, despite the New Testament description of what the Church was up to. In this search for what role I could play in these issues I was reading Ron Sider's classic book, *Rich Christians in an Age of Hunger.* In his book Sider points out that roughly 30,000 children die every day from hunger and preventable diseases.[7] Until I was holding my son that night, that huge number was just a number. But that night I broke. I realized that just that day 30,000 parents watched their son or daughter die because they weren't able to provide their child what I had just provided my son in the last hour. 30,000 families are grief-stricken each day because they didn't win the geographical lottery of where they were born. 30,000 lost their children yesterday, today, and will tomorrow again.

That night became a defining moment when I realized I couldn't help but spend my life acting on the storm of discontent that had been brewing in my soul. My wife and I came to the realization that we had no choice. But even more, the Church as a whole has no choice but to act on this same crisis. These were just some of the defining moments of what would become the birth of an organization that would hold out the vision of a Church that changes the world.

The Role of Personal Vision in Change

Any hope of corporate transformation that does not have at its root individual leadership and responsibility for living out the change is only a well-meaning intention or merely academic discussion. Nothing changes unless the individuals, who are part of a group, change. Already, you may be thinking something like, "I'm not in a position to address global poverty and suffering. I'm not a pastor of a mega-church or in a position to influence the Church. I'm never going to be in a key political role to affect social policy. These issues are too huge and complex for me to play any significant role in them." If any of these statements are reflective of your thoughts or feelings so far, welcome to the club. I would encourage you to keep reading.

If you have a heartbeat, I would strongly argue that you are a leader. You may not have a position or title that is traditionally associated with a leadership role. Or, like God's servants Moses, Gideon, and David, you may assume that you are under-qualified, under-resourced, under-educated, and under-experienced to make a valuable contribution to some of the world's most pressing problems. I'm sure the world's great needs feel like an ocean of suffering next to the cup of water of your individual resources.

However, the follower of Christ who is being fashioned into His image by the power of the Holy Spirit will become more and more attractive to those who assign no value to what they perceive as empty, organized religion. Among the many definitions of the word "leadership," one of the most practical and biblical is simply this: leadership is influence. When you are influencing someone, you are leading. As we will discover in more detail later, when you become like Christ you can't help but influence those around you, just as Christ did. As you are influencing those around you, you are leading them. The choice we make every day as individuals is whether or not to influence people positively or negatively. Parenting, small talk around the water cooler at work, running into a neighbor at the grocery store, or a family dinner, some of the most common and mundane interactions, are opportunities for influence and opportunities to lead.

What does individual servant leadership have to do with the problems of spiritual and physical poverty? Everything. The kind of transformation you will read about here, the kind of change for which the Church and the world is desperate, is totally dependent on decisions you and I make as individuals to experience and reflect the person of Jesus. Abdicating personal servant leadership and simply waiting for our pastors and politicians to initiate corporate change will result in more of the same: all talk and no walk. The revolutionary potential that exists as you and I influence by serving those next door and those on the other side of the world would result in a wave of changed lives, communities, and nations all pointing to the unmistakable existence of our God.

Sadly, most Christians today view the Christian life as "accepting Jesus as their personal Lord and Savior" and then trying their hardest to observe disciplines and rituals which often have no significant biblical basis. It seems that most Christians have grown up in a religious environment where our emotional and spiritual energy was spent trying to avoid specific behavior to perpetuate a pious and morally superior image. Not only have we made following Christ look boring and irrelevant, we have done so while ignoring the greater issues which are actually supposed to be what followers of Jesus are known for addressing. This common condition is ripe for the fruit that results from both individual and corporate servant leadership. It's time we were known for our power instead of our passivity. Not power that comes from position, affluence, title, or superiority, but transforming power that results from servitude.

If we are to become a Church that could transform the world, we must first recover the role that servanthood has in influence. Near the end of Jesus' life and ministry, those who had lived and worked closest to Him started to fight among themselves because they confused power with position. Even after three years of mentoring and discipleship, Jesus' inner circle lost the humility that gave them their transformational influence. Confusing the Kingdom of God with a political kingdom, the mother of James and John saw an opportunity to vie for special positions for her sons. It seems as if James and John put their mother up to asking Jesus for places of honor. Maybe they thought it would go over better if their mom asked. But when the rest of the disciples heard what they had asked they were furious.

So Jesus called them all together for a chat and gave them a little compare and contrast lesson in servant leadership. He essentially told them they were acting like all the other political leaders and rulers who wanted everyone to see that they were above everyone else. They led by position and control. Then He said, *"But among you it will be different. Whoever wants to be a leader among you, must be your servant, and whoever wants to be first among you must become your slave."* Then using Himself as the example, He said, *"For even the Son of Man came not to be served but to serve others and to give his life as a ransom for many"* (Matthew 20:20-28). To live a life that will display the power to influence those around us, our single minded quest must be to emulate the Servant King. The foundational context and assumption of a Church that could transform the world is a Church that would serve the world.

One more note before you read on. My sincere hope is that this book will play a role in leading to transformation among followers of Christ and, in turn, transformation around the world. If these words only engage the intellect and don't impact the core values that determine our behavior, this will have been a waste of time and paper. On the other hand, those serious about living out the implications of these changes will quickly realize that it will take the sustained response of individuals, families, and communities. To enable you to begin to take these thoughts and turn them into action, I have included some "So now what?" questions at the end of each chapter. They can be used for further personal reflection, for a group setting, or both.

My prayer for you as you read and think on these truths is the same as the well known Franciscan benediction:

May God bless you with discomfort
At easy answers, half-truths, and superficial relationships
So that you may live deep within your heart.
May God bless you with anger
At injustice, oppression, and exploitation of people,
So that you may work for justice, freedom, and peace.
May God bless you with tears
To shed for those who suffer pain, rejection, hunger and war,
So that you may reach out your hand to comfort them and
To turn their pain into joy.
And may God bless you with enough foolishness
To believe that you can make a difference in the world,
So that you can do what others claim cannot be done
To bring justice and kindness to all our children and the poor.
Amen[8]

PART ONE – INJUSTICE OF THE GLOBAL IMBALANCE

Chapter 1

How Badly We're Broken

A World and a Church Gone Wrong

I feel like I'm watching a movie. As I look out the window of the Toyota Land Cruiser, driving through Kabul streets, the scenes of a war-torn country are far beyond my version of "normal." Building after bombed out apartment building, bullet ridden telephone poles, and mortar shells embedded in a destroyed movie theater; all look like something Hollywood might bring into my living room whenever I ask it to. However, this is no movie and none of the people are actors. As I watch Afghanis carry out their daily business of buying bread, getting in and out of taxis, and just walking to who knows where, it is hard to fathom that they have all lived through this destruction and devastation.

As we drive down a busy street on our way to visit another needy project site, I see a father sitting on a small piece of tattered cardboard – his only protection from the hot pavement – holding three of his children. All three children look barely conscious. Their clothes are smoggy grey, they wear no shoes, their hair is matted and caked with mud, and their father holds out his hat at anyone who passes by, hoping that the next person might be able to provide the smallest amount of food for his family. My eyes are fixed on him as we drive by and I wonder, "What lottery did I win that that isn't me and my children? What prevents that reality from being the lot that I drew?"

Earlier that same year I traveled in another Toyota Land Cruiser, this time in Santa Cruz, Bolivia. We stopped at a stoplight late one evening coming back from visiting another under-funded project as a very small girl, no more than three or four years old, approaches the vehicle in front of ours begging for anything that might come from inside. My eye catches hers as I sit in the safety of the vehicle and she wanders through the danger of busy traffic. Again, the same painful thought goes through my soul, "What prevents my four year old daughter from being that child? Why is it that I am not living in a slum somewhere forcing my preschool princess to walk through city traffic after dark to beg for coins?" The risk of exploitation and danger is worth the potential that she might come home with a few coins from an ashtray. The stark realities of these painfully wrong situations caused me to ask deeper, more systemic questions: questions that at first shines the spotlight into the dark places of evil and of organized religion's atrophy and apparent inability to respond, but also questions that, if answered and addressed, could bring incredible hope that screams to the world that maybe our news really is good news and just maybe we *can* actually affect global change.

Does God love children from developed nations more than children from developing countries? No! Is the God of the Bible the type of deity that requires a fatalistic response to injustice? Not the One I know. How can a benevolent, loving God condone this type of suffering and injustice?

While my theological training can provide me with a moderately acceptable theological answer to the nature and character of a loving God and humanity's fallen condition, the attractive descriptions of God's love and compassion cause an even greater anger and frustration. The more I understand the incredible compassion and compulsion of God to demonstrate an incomprehensible love for His creation, the more incensed I get that this love doesn't seem to be understood by a world so desperate for its understanding.

For the past century our evangelistic efforts have included statements about "*for God so loved the world*" (John 3:16), yet the world suffers from an embarrassingly gross imbalance of basic resources. Inevitably, questions about the reality of God's love become questions about our inability to demonstrate that love.

Why is it that the Christian religion is not making a difference in the world proportionate to the love we claim to understand and commensurate to the resources that we currently have been "blessed" with? Why, at a time in church history where the organized Christian religion possesses the greatest accumulation of resources ever, is it also true that thousands of children needlessly die each and every day from hunger?

To the ever-growing crowd of religious critics and antagonists, I have an increasingly hard time disagreeing with their observations and conclusions. Looking from the outside in at organized religion would cause even the most gracious observer to move to that of a hostile opponent. We quickly preach a Jesus who fed the hungry multitudes, healed the sick, and revealed the value of the marginalized, yet at the same time we demonstrate a religious system that condones global injustice by our silence and materialistic participation. Instead of being known as a force of love and compassion, as was our founder, we are instead known more by our fractured stance against a handful of moral issues.

Although these issues are not insignificant, my point is that the whole council of Scripture deals much more with concerns over poverty, injustice, and a lack of compassion than it does with the issues that Christians are known today for championing. Why is it that we have so quickly flown the flag of a few moral questions while we have ignored the most pressing global issues of our time, issues that Jesus embraced as responsibilities contained in His own job description? Understanding Isaiah 61 as a prophetic job description for Christ himself, the passage says, "*The LORD has anointed me to preach good news to the poor. He has sent me to comfort the brokenhearted, and to proclaim that captives will be released and prisoners will be freed*" (Isaiah 61:1). The Gospels are filled with stories of Jesus living out this prophetic picture of His work.

So, then, why is it that so much of the developing world understands the "Christian" Church of the West to condone and support a war perceived to be about securing our place over Muslims as economic superpowers; to turn a blind eye to sexual immortality and promiscuity; to sell out to materialistic priorities, while so much of the rest of the world suffers? Simply put, why don't we act like the Jesus we say we follow? Why is it that the world can't see Jesus through our institutional religious system?

Against the backdrop of a global crisis we are perceived as powerless to address comes a hope and an anticipation of a revolution. Out of our comatose hypocrisy, the Sprit of God is awakening His body to move out into a suffering world to be the hands and feet of Jesus. We live in an age where a humiliated Church combined with strategic possibilities, where information about the world's suffering combined with unprecedented resources, and where a spiritual bankruptcy combined with a physical bankruptcy has positioned the followers of Jesus to renovate His Church and reclaim an Acts 2 picture as a force of love and compassion in this world: *"A deep sense of awe came over them all, and the apostles performed many miraculous signs and wonders. And all the believers met together in one place and shared everything they had. They sold their property and possessions and shared the money with those in need"* (Acts 2:43-45).

It is toward this hope for change that this book confronts the injustice of the global imbalance of resources and then compares it to a Biblical vision of a compassionate Church. After looking at what I believe is idealistically and wonderfully possible we will then examine what I believe are the core value changes that must take place if we are to see a renovated Church that can affect the unprecedented alleviation of needless suffering.

Out of This Crazy World

Humor me. Imagine for a few minutes that the Mars exploration projects discovered that there was actually intelligent life on the red planet. Let's pretend that the Mars rover bumped into a little green man or woman (because we're not sure how to tell them apart yet). Lo and behold we then find out that Martians are advanced in space travel, and we invite them to come to Earth to learn about humans and life on our planet. We would be proud to show them what we have accomplished in the past few thousand years and why Earth is the best place in the solar system to live.

The big day finally comes. After an unprecedented reception at NASA, the leader of the Martian team is welcomed by the President of the United States and the two have a meeting at the White House. (Stay with me here.)

Shortly into the conversation the Martian leader comments, "Life on your planet must be very good if you have the ability to explore other planets and the far away galaxies."

"Yes," comments the President with great pride, "Western civilization is the most advanced it has ever been. So much so that we are exploring new galaxies and making incredible achievements in space travel. In fact, I have just budgeted over 18 billion dollars to continue our work in seeking intelligent life on other planets, looking further and further into space."[9] The Martian is very impressed and says to the President, "I assume, then, that everyone on your planet must have enough food to eat every day?" The President pauses for a moment, confused by the sudden switch in topic. "Well, not quite. Actually about 6 million children die each year of starvation."[10]

"Oh," says the Martian, "then you must not have enough food on your planet to feed all of your people."

"No. Actually we have more than enough food. In fact just 2% of the world's grain harvest would be enough, if shared, to feed the entire planet."[11]

"Oh, I see," the Martian replies, a bit more confused, "then I assume you don't have the ability to get food to all of the people who are hungry."

"No," says the President. His demeanor is now a little more modest. "In reality, we have great railways, vast transportation systems, huge ships, and cargo planes."

"Oh…" says the Martian, even more perplexed. This time the little green man remains quiet with a pensive and furrowed look on his face. He is obviously trying to make sense of what the President is saying. After a few uncomfortable moments, the President speaks up with a distinct air of defensiveness. "Well, you see, the issues of global poverty are complex. It takes great amounts of cooperation and determination and large amounts of funding to address the global imbalance of resources."

"Let me get this straight," replies the Martian, "just today, and every day, about 16,000 of your most vulnerable inhabitants died just because they don't have enough food to eat. Yet you grow enough food to feed the entire population of your planet hundreds of times over and you even have the ability to get the food to those who need it. But instead, you choose to spend billions of dollars working on what I can only assume is the incredibly complex and coordinated job of sending your people and equipment into space to see what is out there?"

If I were the Martian, I would get back into my flying saucer and go back to Mars and never let an Earthling step foot onto my planet.

Have I oversimplified the problem? Maybe I have. The issue of poverty, and its causes, *are* very complex. However, it is clear that whether we are talking about the choices of a person or of a country, the global imbalance of the most fundamental life-sustaining resources tells us that we act out and express to the world that our comfort and our interests are more important than the basic survival of other people. We would never admit it in so many words, but those in the developing world have heard that message loud and clear.

Now to a real life story. A few of years ago, I was in Nigeria helping to establish a rural hospital. We had the privilege of working with a group of people in Western Canada, who had a vision to open a hospital in Nigeria that would prevent mothers from unnecessarily dying during childbirth. This group had donated funds to build some buildings, but needed some assistance in getting their health center up and running. We spent a lot of time consulting and involving heath care professionals, and working with the rural community leaders and local health authorities in Nigeria. Our plan was to slowly begin out-patient primary care services, building on those services with a maternity program as funds became available. As with most international development projects, our plans included community consultations in order to, among other purposes, manage the expectations of the people. Many women and children were dying because of either poor or inadequate maternal health care. In fact, the initial vision of the hospital was to address the devastation of maternal and infant death in the surrounding communities.

11

Shortly after we had established out-patient services, I traveled back to Nigeria to evaluate the project and plan for the next phase. During the two-week trip, one of the local pastors comes on his motorbike to visit with us one evening. I had gotten to know this pastor very well on previous trips. He constantly has a smile on his face that reveals a joy that eludes most; knowing him and the challenges he faces in caring for his people, it is an encouragement just to spend time around him. We start talking about the hospital project and the expectations of his community. At the time, I'm thinking it's a strategic opportunity to reinforce the realities of the challenges of fundraising in Canada and the principle that donor groups need to see the results of the initial out-patient services before we could raise the funds for maternity services. As I talk he keeps smiling and nodding. I think I'm doing a commendable job in cross-cultural expectation management.

As I finish talking, the pastor, with that same magical smile on his face, asks me a question I will never forget: "Brother, in your country do you have hospitals for your pets?" After a long pause and some quick thinking I am only left with the truth. "Yes," I reply, "we do." Still smiling, my African friend goes on to say, "We cannot understand such a thing. We cannot understand why you can so easily have hospitals for your dogs, yet it is such a difficult thing for you to raise funds to help us with a place to safely deliver our children."

Without going down the possibly defensible rabbit trail of animal rights (no pun intended) and the benefits of owning pets, the value contrast was painful and the lesson sobering. My friend's comments didn't make the challenges of fundraising any less daunting; however, his observations were, at the very least, an incredibly helpful perspective on the difficulty in managing the expectations of his people. More so, his comments became a moment that has been burned in my mind and heart to help me begin to understand the injustice of the global imbalance of resources and Western priorities.

Maybe like the President in the fictional story of the Martian, the very real story of the conversation with my African friend caused me to stand embarrassed at the reality of what his illustration was pointing out. And even worse was the veracity that I stood before him as another Christian leader, representing a Western Church with access to unprecedented resources and opportunities to meet this most basic, yet unmet, need.

Chapter 1 - So now what?

1. Which statements about a world and a Church gone wrong do you agree with or disagree with?

2. How do people around you view the Church or religion?

3. What do you think the Western Church (Western Europe and North America) is known for today and why?

4. What thoughts or feelings emerged as you read the fictitious story of the Martian coming to Earth?

5. What did you think of the questions the Martian had for the President?

6. What thoughts or feelings emerged as you read the real story of my discussion with the Nigerian pastor? Do you think it was fair or legitimate for the Nigerian pastor to question me the way he did?

7. What are some of the parallels between the stories of the Martian and the Nigerian pastor?

8. Why do you think that North Americans are generally ambivalent toward the degree of suffering that is the reality for half of the world's population?

Chapter 2

The Picture of Their Physical Poverty

Real People

I fully understand the problem of discussing statistics is that it can leave us focused on numbers and not people. Far beneath the macro-picture of poverty, we *must* come face to face with the real people it plagues. We are motivated not by numbers, but by a life we can identify with. So let me begin by telling you about one life.

Just days before writing this chapter, I received an email from one of our staff who was leading a medical team to Haiti, the poorest country in the western hemisphere. Haiti is just over an hour's flight from Florida, but despite its proximity to one of the richest countries in the world, the people of Haiti suffer unbelievable poverty. That day, I was told that the team had treated a newborn baby girl who had been found abandoned, barely alive, under a bridge. With her umbilical cord still attached, she was found being eaten alive by an army of ants.

With the email came a photo of a tiny, precious baby girl with red open welts all over her body, obvious signs of the torturous first hours of her life. The man who found her named her Elizabeth. We don't know the specifics of the situation or why she had been abandoned, but Elizabeth was probably left under a bridge because her mother was simply too destitute to provide her with the basics of life. Throwing her away, like the week's garbage, would have been less painful than watching her suffer a poverty-induced death. Thank God that, in His sovereignty, He saw fit to save this little one from dying. However, around the world each day some 30,000 children under the age of 5 aren't as lucky as Elizabeth and die for the same inexcusable reason that almost took her life: poverty.

As I sit here thinking and writing about Elizabeth, I am filled with a mixture of sadness and anger. The only real difference between Elizabeth and the 30,000 children who *did* die in the past 24 hours is that I happened to find out *her* name and I happened to see *her* picture. As you think with me about the numbers, the facts, and the figures of poverty and global imbalance, they represent people like Elizabeth and her mother.

Real Numbers

Since 1990, the commonly used "$1 a day" classification describes someone who lives in extreme or absolute poverty.[1] More recently, new World Bank policy research suggests that $1.25 should be the new global standard for measuring extreme or absolute poverty.[2] At this new threshold, 1.4 billion people in the world live in extreme poverty.[3] Using a 2005 world population of approximately 6.5 billion people,[4] more than 20% of the world population suffers the effects of absolute poverty. However, this is only the beginning of the daily tragedy: while a fifth of the world's people are *extremely* poor, almost half of the world population, more than 2.5 billion people, is considered to suffer the effects of poverty, living on less that $2 a day.[5]

Before you protest, "It costs less to live in these countries anyway, so these numbers really don't mean anything," understand that these measurements of purchasing power and poverty lines have been adjusted for parity in the United States. Therefore, to understand what living on less than $1 would be like, imagine what it would be like to live on less than $30 a month in the United States. Try to fathom providing food, clothing, shelter, schooling and health care for yourself on $30 a month, or $360 a year, in the US!

It is impossible to really know exactly how many people suffer needlessly from hunger or poverty related issues. Different sources quote different numbers and yearly disasters, war, politics, and economic shifts change the numbers. What we can say with certainty is that roughly one billion people today endure the injustice and pain of abject poverty, and another two billion are poor.

Let's go beyond official poverty lines and look at many of the other measurable effects of poverty and preventable diseases:

- Globally, nearly 10 million children under the age of five die each year (approximately 27,000 per day) from hunger and easily preventable causes. Putting that into perspective, at that rate it would take only three and a half years to wipe out the entire population of Canada, the country in which I live.

- 27,000 children dying every day would be the equivalent to one Asian Tsunami every week or about 100 passenger planes crashing every day, yet it hardly ever makes the news.

- 6 million children die each year from malnutrition and starvation alone.[6]

- 852 million people in the world are hungry, and 300 million people in the world are obese.[7]

- Almost one billion people in the world cannot read or sign their own name.[8]

- Based on enrollment data in 2005 about 72 million primary school age children were not in school.[9] In many countries, far fewer girls than boys attend school. Economic disparity encourages gender disparity.

- 20% of the world's population in developed countries consumes 80% of all the world's resources, which means that 80% of the world's population, from the poorest countries, are left to live off of 20% of the world's resources.[10] Also, stop and think about the fact that the 20% of us who are consuming the vast majority of the world's resources are from Canada, the United States, Western Europe, and Australia, countries that over the past 100 years were known as "Christian" countries, established on biblical principles. In light of the current geo-religious realities, might there be a legitimate case to argue the corporate mass hypocrisy of the Western Church?

- The poorest 20% of the world's population is trying to survive on 1.5% of the world's resources.[11] Should this have any bearing on our daily consumption choices?

- For every $1 that is spent on official development assistance, $25 is spent on debt repayment by developing countries.[12]

- By 2010 UNICEF predicts that there will be more than 15 million children just from sub-Saharan Africa alone who have been orphaned by HIV/AIDS.[13]

- In 2007, the number of people who died of AIDS was equal to twenty 747 passenger jets crashing daily.[14]

- In Africa, a child dies every 30 seconds from malaria, an easily preventable and treatable disease.[15]

- At any given time, half of all hospital beds in the world are occupied because of water-borne diseases.[16]

- 3.5 million people die each year from water-borne diseases; 84% of these are under the age of 14.[17]

- Less than 1% of the world's fresh water supply is readily accessible for human use.[18]

Some Faces Behind the Numbers

In May of 2005, I conducted a project assessment trip in the Siaya District of western Kenya. I had been confronted by poverty and its effects many times before on many trips, but this day I saw the addition of HIV/AIDS to poverty's usual toll. Visiting some potential project sites, I walked down a path right by a church and an orphan home. As we climbed over a barbed fence and walked through tall corn stalks, we came upon four round mud huts with thatched grass roofs. Six to eight foot corn stalks surrounded each of the huts. As we came upon the first hut we met an old woman. She looked like she was in her seventies. She is just one of the 1.4 billion people who try to live on less than $1.25 a day. Even at first glance she looked extremely poor. Her clothes were all torn and very dirty. She wasn't wearing shoes, but the soles of her feet looked like the soles of my shoes. It was obvious that other things were more of a priority than shoes. We asked her about her life and her current situation. The four huts belonged to four widows; they all lived in a compound of sorts. Each widow had been a wife of the same man. Their mud huts were falling apart. Termites ate away at the sticks that provided the support for the mud walls. Then we were told that two of the homes were made not with mud but with cow manure. You see, they said, walls of dung were stronger than walls made just of mud. They considered themselves lucky to have a home made from manure that could withstand the heavy African rainfalls. As we entered one of the thatched huts it became obvious that manure made up a significant part of the walls.

As we continued to talk, she then went on to tell us that all four widows had lost all of their children and grandchildren to AIDS. Their families were completely wiped out by the pandemic. I asked where everyone was buried, and she pointed to the corn fields. We walked only a few steps away from their home and we could see many piles of dirt with corn growing out of the ground. Each pile of dirt was a grave. They had run out of room to bury their families so some of them were buried right next to their homes. One of the widows pointed to a short grave, telling us that is where her granddaughter was buried. Through our interpreter the woman then told me she didn't want to talk about family anymore because it was too painful. With no one to take care of them, they went days without anything to eat. Their health was very poor and even if they had money to pay a doctor, they lived too far to walk to a clinic.

We sat with them for a while and listened to them tell us more about their lives. As I sat in their world listening to their stories, I couldn't help but think of how absolutely wrong the situation was. I was comparing my world, at home in Canada, to theirs. And I was sick with the thought of how different our lives were. Four hungry and sick old widows, living in huts made with cow excrement, whose children and grandchildren were all dead from AIDS, buried in shallow graves that now grew the corn that feeds them for only 3 months of the year. I couldn't handle the thought of my own Grandma living here – like this.

Almost immobilized by the immensity of their pain, and knowing there was little I could do or give to address the depth of their need, I asked if they knew Jesus. Two of them said they became born again when the church was built next to their huts. They smiled as they talked about Him. One of them asked me for a hospital, which kind of made me smile. I told them that I would do two things: pray for them right there and that I would come back with food. First I prayed, and it was completely humbling to hear them agree with me that God was a provider and a healer. If they could have faith that God could do this, I can never question Him again.

Then we went and bought each of them a bag of food that would last them about a week. I wanted to buy them more, but we were told that if we did, it would be stolen anyway. When we came back, I explained that the food was from God and that somehow He hadn't forgotten about them. They smiled thankfully and nodded in agreement. I had the distinct impression they believed what I was saying more than I did.

Comparing the Numbers

Most of us have heard these kinds of numbers and stories before. And, as I already mentioned, reading big numbers can perpetuate the mind and heart numbing condition that contributes to symptoms of apathy. Rarely, however, do we hold up the economic realities and injustices in the developing world against the backdrop of conventional Western living and economics. The conclusions reveal an even more damning commentary on the real values of those of us in the West.

Before the comparison, I want us to be reminded of one statement Jesus made about economics. In Luke 12, which we will examine in more detail later, Jesus was teaching His followers about hypocritical living, warning against the way the religious leaders lived. As He went on to teach specifically about money and possessions, Jesus said, *"Wherever your treasure is, there the desires of your heart will also be"* (Luke 12:34). What we individually or corporately use our money for is the clearest window through which to see the true priorities and values of our lives. Now, in comparison to the economics of poverty and the costs of development, let's take a look at what we really value.

More than 10 years ago, UNICEF estimated that the cost of providing the basics of life for everyone on Earth (nutrition, education, clean water, health, etc.) would take an additional $40 billion a year on top of what is already being spent on social development.[19] Essentially, if someone wanted to come along and pick up the tab right now to eradicate needless suffering, the price tag would be in the neighborhood of $40 billion a year. The essentials would be broken down something like this, in USD per year:[20]

- Basic education for all: $6 billion

- Clean water and sanitation for all: $9 billion

- Reproductive health for all women: $12 billion

- Basic health and nutrition: $13 billion

Does $40 billion sound like a lot of money? Let's compare that with some other big spending numbers (USD per year):

- US military spending: $650 billion[21]

- Canadian military spending: $15 billion[22]

- World golf spending: $40 billion[23]

- Dieting programs in the US: $40 billion[24]

- Aesthetic cosmetic surgeries and procedures in the US: $11 billion[25]

- US advertising expenses in 2002: $237 billion[26]

- Online pornography revenue worldwide in 2006: $97 billion[27]

- Cosmetics in the US: $8 billion[28]

- Ice Cream in Europe: $11 billion[29]

- Global spending on ringtones and ringtunes in 2005: $3.8 billion[30]

- Projected global spending on mobile phone games, music, and video in 2010: $43 billion[31]

- Perfume in Europe and the US: $12 billion[32]

- Pet food in Europe and the US: $17 billion[33]

- Cigarettes in Europe: $50 billion[34]

- Worth of real estate owned by institutional churches in the US: $230 billion[35]

- Given by Christians to church buildings: $9 - 11 billion a year[36]

- New church construction in the US between 1984-1989: $15.7 billion[37]

- Church income worldwide in 2007: $150 billion[38]

- Para-church and Christian institutional income worldwide in 2007: $240 billion[39]

- Stolen by church leaders in 2007: $24 billion[40]

- Additional church income if all US church members tithed (10%) on reported income: $164 billion[41]

- Total being spent on development to developing countries in 2004: $78 billion[42]

If you are like me, you'll find there is a significant degree of disconnect with numbers like this. No matter how much we might give intellectual assent to the injustice of the obvious global imbalance of resources, no one person ever reading this will likely be in a position to affect significant change in something like US military spending or the amount spent on cigarettes in Europe. We feel helpless to affect the kind of macro change that could quickly bring about justice and equity around the globe.

However, it is abundantly clear: if Jesus is right about our hearts being where our money is, we don't have a priority for compassion or for the change that is needed to alleviate needless suffering. As a global citizen, my individual choices about what I do or don't do with my money contribute to many of these numbers. Furthermore, our governments and policy makers at least claim to make decisions and form policies that line up with the values of those who elect them. Knowingly or unknowingly, we agree with these priorities by our vote or our silence. If the majority of those who paid taxes and cast ballots in the Western world really cared about needless suffering, for certain these numbers would be different.

I am not suggesting for a moment that personal spending in all of these areas is inherently wrong, nor am I judging the practical realities that necessitate spending in some of these areas. In fact, healthy spirituality enables us to enjoy what God has blessed us with. My point, however, is twofold: first, we already have more than enough financial resources to see needless suffering eradicated; and second, global imbalance and current financial priorities are indicative of a deep spiritual decay in the West that must be addressed if we are to see a world transformed.

Just for a moment, imagine how the world might be different today if, since September 11, 2001, the US spent only 10% of its military budget on relief and development. Averaged over the past 8 years, that would amount to an addition of more than

$50 billion per year being invested in development:[43] more than enough to provide the basics of life to every human on the planet. If courageous, visionary decisions like that were made, the world would be different today and global attitudes and positions on US foreign policy would be radically different than they currently are.

I am not a foreign policy or security expert, but I would even propose that the most effective way to have fought a global war on terror over the past decade would have been to fight a global war on poverty and injustice. I would also venture to speculate that terrorist and extremist leaders would dramatically lose their following and the voice to mobilize attacks against nations that, in an unprecedented fashion, provided clean water, sufficient nutrition, education to their children, and proper health care. Instead of a coalition of the willing to use military force to fight an ideology of hate, if there was a coalition of the willing to fight the injustice of economic disparity and needless suffering, I am convinced that hatred for the West would silently crumble on the heap of other failed ideologies.

Idealistic? Very possible. Naively simplistic? Also very possible. However, what do we have to lose? What we have done over the past decade obviously has not produced a safer, more peaceful world for us all to live in. We obviously haven't beaten our adversaries with the might of our military. If anything, we have fueled more hatred for the West and given even more justification for them to target us. Just maybe, over the next decades, we can beat our enemies with the might of our coordinated corporate compassion.

Right now, the Muslim world looks at the "Christian" West and, in the absence of contrary proof, equates our Christianity with our corporate policies and spending priorities. While millions in the Middle East and South and Central Asia continue to suffer extreme poverty, what they see of "Christian" nations is that we keep fighting a war that is perceived to be fought against their religion. We pour billions of dollars every year into fighting them while their children die from hunger and a lack of clean water. Not only have we demonstrated to the world the antithesis of the Jesus we say we follow (which is corporate hypocrisy on a historical level), but we have also given them even more reason to be incensed by our very existence.

A friend of mine is a pastor of a very unconventional church that looks for every way possible to communicate and demonstrate the love of Christ. His congregation is in a large, multi-cultural community that contains a large number of recent immigrants. His vision was to specifically buy a building that was to be used as a community center, providing whatever services were needed to people transitioning to life in their new country. On the weekends he would also use the facility to hold Sunday services. With the assistance of a foundation, they purchased a building and went about providing all kinds of social services to anyone who needed them. For example, they tutored kids who needed help, they taught English lessons, and they provided life and employment skills for immigrants.

As the Arabic and South Asian communities came to know about the center and its services, they approached this pastor and asked if they could use the facility to hold prayer services on Fridays; the Muslim holy day. Realizing that their building was not sacred, and that they were committed to building relationships to communicate the love of Christ in any way possible, my friend agreed to allow the Muslim community to worship in his building on Fridays and also continued to meet to worship Christ on Sundays. Because Friday is a work day for this pastor, he takes time to greet Muslims as they come to Friday prayers. It is this kind of unconditional compassion that reveals the character of Christ and can change the world.

Morally Bankrupt

Peter Singer, the Princeton ethicist, presented the following moral dilemma in his most recent book, *The Life You Can Save*:

> On your way to work, you pass a small pond. On hot days, children sometimes play in the pond, which is only about knee-deep. The weather's cool today, though, and the hour is early, so you are surprised to see a child splashing about in the pond. As you get closer, you see that it is a very young child, just a toddler, who is flailing

about, unable to stay upright or walk out of the pond. You look for the parents or the babysitter, but there is no one else around. The child is unable to keep his head above the water for more than a few seconds at a time. If you don't wade in and pull him out, he seems likely to drown. Wading in is easy and safe, but you will ruin your new shoes you bought only a few days ago, and get your suit wet and muddy. By the time you hand the child over to someone responsible for him, and change your clothes, you'll be late for work. What should you do?[44]

This specific moral dilemma is, of course, hypothetical. Yet its parallel reality is extremely real and the lesson is extremely accurate. I don't know of one person for whom this dilemma is complex. The solution is obvious. The life of that one child is obviously worth the cost of a new pair of shoes and a suit and worth the inconvenience of our time. However, while we would all agree to the right or most moral course of action in Singer's hypothetical dilemma, most of us live out the opposite reality day after day. As we have discovered, while we easily have all the resources needed to eradicate extreme suffering, saving the lives of 10 million children each year, we simply choose to not help. Like the man on his way to work, our actions reveal that we would rather not wreck a new pair of shoes and a suit and be inconvenienced in our daily lives, than save the life that is before us. There is no other conclusion than that we care more about our luxuries than their lives. The only difference between the hypothetical dilemma and the thousands of children who died today is that it didn't happen before our eyes.

As dark and disparaging as these truths are, the numbers also tell us something wonderfully hopeful. The eradication of extreme suffering is a dream that is simply within reach. Without having to give up all that we enjoy, if those who call themselves Christians became minimally obedient with our resources, and gave more money and time to help people rise out of poverty, we could handily provide the basics of survival for everyone on earth. Singer puts it this way:

> A modest contribution from everyone who has enough to live comfortably, eat out occasionally, and buy bottled water, would suffice to achieve the goal of lifting most of the world's extremely poor people above the poverty line of $1.25 a day. If that modest contribution were given, we would no longer be in a situation in which 10 million children were dying from poverty each year.[45]

The fact is, we who are from developed nations, could eradicate extreme suffering without at all putting ourselves or the well being of our own children at risk.

We must become much more concerned about living out the love of Christ in our efforts to be right. While the numbers, statistics, and measurements of global economic inequality and financial priorities reveal that there are more than enough resources to transform the world, they also cast a spotlight on the moral and spiritual deficiency in the developed world. That leads us into our next chapter.

Chapter 2 - So now what?

1. Was there a specific story that caused you to think of poverty in a new way and if so, how?

2. Which statistics and facts are "news" to you?

3. Which statistics or facts made the greatest impression on you? Why?

4. What is your reaction to the comparison between the cost to eradicate extreme suffering and the global spending priorities apparent today?

5. Why do you think extreme suffering exists alongside unprecedented wealth?

6. If your children where chronically hungry, and your neighbor was extremely wealthy, how might you feel about your neighbor over time?

7. What is your response to Peter Singer's hypothetical moral dilemma? Do you think it's an accurate parallel to the current injustice of the global imbalance of resources and our apathy?

Chapter 3

The Picture of Our Spiritual Poverty

There Has Got to be More Than This

We can't examine the macro picture of suffering, injustice, and resource distribution without asking some serious questions about the condition of our own spiritual house first. As I previously pointed out, it is those of us from the developed world, who are predominantly and historically from Christian nations, who are consuming 80% of the world's resources. While it is widely recognized that Western countries can not officially be considered "Christian" any longer, no one can dispute the biblical values and practices that contributed to the foundations of Western Europe, Canada and the United States.

History confirms that the Church, in its various forms, played a vital role in establishing Western civilization. One doesn't have to read history books for very long before the Christian roots of Western civilization become evident. Most civil leaders claim a faith based in Christian tradition, and it is not uncommon to see politicians still evoking the name or blessing of God in their speeches or in their leadership. Photo ops of leaders walking in and out of churches, or publically seeking the council of recognized spiritual leaders, is still at least politically, if not spiritually, advantageous.

While church growth in many developing countries is dramatically exceeding that in the West, much of the developing world still perceives Christianity to be the religion of the West or the "white man's faith." Therefore we can't escape the reality that woefully inadequate foreign relief and development policy and practice is at least the "ugly step sister" of the Western Church, if not a pretty accurate reflection of the Church's foreign policies and practices. Either way, our personal and corporate financial priorities reveal a spiritual and moral decay that exacerbates the injustice of resource use.

A Deeper Look at the Real Problem

Pulling back only a few religious layers reveals an internal catatonic state of the Church in the West that is often more apparent to those outside than those on the inside. Much is currently being written about the ineffectiveness or irrelevance of the North American Church and more than a few are proposing a revolution that must take place. I join with the many who are calling for there to be a real awakening in the Western Church and a re-engagement in a world of searing suffering. My intent here is simply to paint a picture in order to demonstrate the direct link of spiritual transformation to social transformation. To make an important distinction, it is not the *nature* of Church that is broken or deficient, just our interpretation and manifestation of it.

As I will demonstrate later, no faith system or worldview has a greater responsibility and opportunity to address the issues of needless suffering and poverty than that of the followers of Christ. Within its very essence, there is a fundamental expectation that *Christ*ians would be like *Christ*. However, we hear time and time again about the general irrelevance of the Church and the perception that Christians are very un-Christ like. This constant judgment has consistent irrefutable proof.

Again, the truth that the wallet is a window to the heart's priorities gives us the first clue that we as Christians have conformed to the pattern of this world. Despite thousands of years of teaching that God's people should be living out an economic reality vastly different than that of the pagans, all dashboard indicators suggest it is we who have once again conformed to the world's values. The following paragraphs are only a few of the most well-known teachings relating to God's people, the poor, and the use of resources.

In an effort to create an environment of equality and discourage an ever-increasing disparity between the rich and poor, God tells

His people in Leviticus 25 that they must return the land (their means of producing wealth) to the families who originally owned it every 50 years. In order to prevent continual subjugation and inequality, God commands His people in Deuteronomy 15 to cancel all debts against each other every seven years. To give the poor the opportunity to gather food, and to give the soil the opportunity to rest, Exodus 23 teaches that they were to leave the land alone for one full year out of every seven.

Deuteronomy 22 teaches that every three years, instead of taking the tithe (or a tenth) of what they produced to the temple as worship, they were to take that entire year's tithe and give it to the widows, orphans, and the poor.

In Acts 2 and 4, the early church modeled these historical teachings by actually selling their lands and homes in order to have resources to help the poor. Amazing!

Today, these teachings would be the radical equivalent - and just as unpopular - of walking into town and saying, "Ok folks, here is what you are going to do with your stuff so that we can eradicate needless suffering and look after all of the AIDS orphans in the world: first, I want everyone to return their farms and business to those families who originally owned them, just in case any of those people are needy. Do that regularly every 50 years. Second, I want all of the businesses to wipe away their accounts receivable and the lenders to erase all debt, mortgages, car payments, and lines of credit every seven years so that people can use that money to help the poor instead of paying you back with interest. Next, every three years, instead of giving any money to your church, take the first 10% of everything you earn and give it the poor or to organizations that help the poor. Oh, and lastly, call your real estate agent. You are going to be selling your homes and land and all your extra stuff, buying smaller homes, simplifying, and using the leftover money to help the poor escape poverty. And with everything else you have left, I want you to share it with those who might need it. There are other instructions I will have later as to how we can give more, but let's just start with that. Alright…so how does that sound to everyone?"

The problem with chuckling and quickly dismissing that message as complete nonsense is that this was exactly what our God commanded His people and wrote down for us to follow. Equality, justice, compassion, and generosity were built into the DNA of the economic and religious systems. However, most don't realize how sick they really are. Those who claim to follow Christ today don't even know these instructions existed and, if they did and were willing to incorporate them into their financial decisions, they wouldn't know where to begin. To twenty-first century Western materialistic, independent people that might sound like ridiculous, socialist extremism. To first century Palestinian, interdependent Jews and Gentiles who had just walked with Jesus, it likely sounded exactly like Him.

Let's now briefly look at some of the realities of what Christians in North America are doing, or not doing, with their money. Despite unprecedented prosperity in the last 70 years, North Americans actually gave more during the Great Depression (3.3% of their income) than they did in 2004 (2.5%).[1] This means the more money we made over the past decades, the less of it we gave away. We should not be surprised by this reality: even a basic understanding of human nature reveals that the more money and possessions we attain, the more self-absorbed we become. Regardless of whether or not you think tithing was abolished as a command in the New Testament, the biblical use of resources would suggest that giving 10% is the place to start, not the ultimate goal of stewardship. However, only 9% of Christians, narrowly defined as evangelical, tithed in 2002.[2] On average, Christian young adults under the age of 35 with a household income of $40,000 – $60,000 only gave 2% of that income to anything charitable.[3]

Our self-imposed corporate spiritual bankruptcy is not only seen in our stewardship of resources, but it is also seen in the general health of our church communities. In Canada in 1946, 67% of Canadians attended weekly services.[4] In 2003, while almost 80% of Canadians agreed that Jesus was the son of God and that God isn't just an old superstition, less than 20% said they attend any regular church service.[5] This tells us that while most say they believe in Jesus, they are not finding Him in our churches.

While more people on average still attend regular church services in the United States, the declining trend is the same. In 2004, only 43% said they attended a service in the past seven days, down from 49% in 1991.[6]

In Western Europe, almost 50% of the population said that God was an important part of their lives, but only 20% indicated that they attended regular services.[7] Beautiful cathedrals and ancient church buildings now stand only as historical monuments to a once influential social force.

Beyond weekly church attendance in the Western world, the personal choices and lifestyles of Christians mirror that of those who claim no faith. In his book, *The Scandal of the Evangelical Conscience*, Ron Sider outlines a sobering evaluation of US evangelicals:

> To say there is a crisis of disobedience in the evangelical world today is to dangerously understate the problem. Born-again Christians divorce at about the same rate as everyone else. Self-centered materialism is seducing evangelicals and rapidly destroying our earlier, slightly more generous giving. Born-again Christians justify and engage in sexual promiscuity (both pre-marital sex and adultery) at astonishing rates. Racism and perhaps

physical abuse of wives seem to be worse in evangelical circles than elsewhere.[8]

Before those of us from outside the United States declare this critique as uniquely American, we need to remember that, in the developed world, it is Americans who still attend regular church services more than citizens of any other industrialized country. If this is the description of "born-again" Christianity in the United States, it is likely that we in Canada and Western Europe are even guiltier of the same judgment.

The Consequences of Our Coma

Sadly, the consequences of our spiritual lethargy are numerous and global. A few years ago, I was speaking with a childhood friend of mine. We used to attend church together, but he has since joined the many who find no value in organized religion, so he stopped going to church. As we spoke he said to me, "I hate religion." It seemed like he was almost looking for a defensive reaction from me. My response surprised and disarmed him. "Me too," I said calmly. Knowing my former career in church work as a pastor, he looked at me as if we were both going to get struck by lightning and said, "Are you allowed to say that?" I went on to share with him that I had a love for Jesus and a passion to mirror the life that He lived, but that I too, hate many of the religious systems that claim His name. My friend completely agreed with me and said that he still reads his Bible. He reads the stories of

Jesus and also wants his life to be like that of Christ. How is it that people could be so attracted to Jesus, who lived more than 2000 years ago, yet want nothing to do with institutionalized Christianity?

Like my friend, I have also watched superstar Christian leaders on TV publicly confess adultery and go to jail for fraud and theft. We have all watched and heard about the many priests who have abused hundreds of children. In Canada, we have had a generation of residential school abuse by churches who forcibly took young children away from their parents and, for years, tried to force them into another culture and religion, in the name of Jesus. Like my friend, I am also sickened by another infomercial of an evangelist trying to sell miracle water to people who can't afford it, also in the name of Jesus. All of this has been broadcasted for the world to see in just the past forty years, while half of the world suffers from easily preventable poverty. Frankly, I'm surprised people aren't leaving the Church faster. Religion has left people empty and hungry, but the reality of the person of Jesus can still shine through our cracked and broken sacred forms. I am not suggesting that the goal is for Christianity to become popular in the social trend sense. I am however convinced that Christ can and must again become attractive to those who see Him reflected in His followers. God's existence will never be empirically, mechanically, or scientifically proven; however,

God's love and power can be made evident every day around the world as we purpose to be the hands and feet of Jesus.

But it's Not Over

It is this hunger for substance that has created an awakening of people who see the incredible potential of a world that could be transformed by a revived and renovated Church. We have a world that is starving for life. People in the affluent West have discovered that possessions and prosperity have not provided the happiness and fulfillment they believed it would; at the same time, there is an institutional Church which is rarely, if at all, sought out by those looking to fill the deepest areas of their souls. Even worse, research and reality tells us that even if people do turn to the Church, they rarely find the Answer to their deepest void. Paralleling this spiritual emptiness and search for personal meaning, the physical deprivation and extreme poverty that exists in the world is becoming a greater global priority. People, spiritually motivated or not, are rediscovering the joy and personal fulfillment that comes from what they give, rather than from what they receive. The conditions are perfect for change. Again, Western Christians already have the physical and spiritual resources necessary to affect unprecedented global change in our generation. We also have a Leader who has already shown us how to do it.

Exploring the depths of the current brokenness of the Western Church, the spiritual emptiness of the affluent 20% of the world's population, and the incomprehensible suffering of over a billion of our poorest inhabitants can quickly leave us discouraged and hopeless. However, I am convinced that the darkness of this night will be offset by the approaching dawn. In stark contrast to the current realities of spiritual and physical poverty, let's capture a biblical vision for what is actually possible.

Chapter 3 - So now what?

1. What has been your experience with "religion"?

2. How is it that your individual spiritual life affects (positively or negatively) the general spiritual temperature of the North American Church?

3. Would you agree or disagree with my general evaluation of the condition of the Western Church? Why or why not?

4. How have you seen the church positively or negatively influence your immediate contacts and situations?

5. What statistics or general state of affairs of the Church concern you the most and why?

6. How would you articulate the difference between being a Christian and being a follower of Jesus?

7. What examples could you give between the difference of religious form and spiritual substance?

8. What would be some of the elements of your spiritual community that would either attract or deter outsiders?

9. What are your general reactions to Part One?

PART TWO – THE BIBLICAL PICTURE
OF A COMPASSIONATE CHURCH

Chapter 4

Christians Are Just a Bunch of Hypocrites

Getting it Right

My good friend Ron owns a small coffee shop in the town we live in. He has a passion for running a business that can be used to impact the lives of the world's poor. He has been on a few international trips with me and his heart is wrecked by the unnecessary suffering of children. Our mutual friend, Mike told me a story about his unbelieving social worker friend who was in the coffee shop one day talking with Ron about some of the situations she was dealing with. As with most social workers, she had many stories of people who needed help in one form or another. She told Ron about a 14-year-old girl she was working with. The girl had come from a very difficult home life and was now in the care of social services. When the social worker mentioned that the girl's birthday was approaching, something or Someone touched Ron's heart and he went out and bought a birthday present for this complete stranger as well as some day-to-day items that a teenage girl might typically receive from caring and loving parents. As Ron requested, the social worker delivered the gift package anonymously, and purposely returned to tell him that the girl was thrilled to receive a present like this. The 14-year-old commented that this was the first birthday present she had ever received.

The social worker was moved by Ron's compassion and was telling Mike about this guy who owned a coffee shop and who did this small but great thing to practically touch this young life. When Mike told her that he actually knew Ron, she then asked, "Is Ron a Christian?" Mike answered that he was. Then she replied with this statement that I think best describes what is truly possible when Christians act like Christ. She said, "Well, if that is what a Christian is, then tell me where to sign up." It was refreshing to hear a story about someone who was actually attracted to Christianity after meeting a Christian.

Getting it Wrong

"Christians are hypocrites!" How many times have we heard that flippant comment from someone who has an axe to grind, legitimately or not? We've all heard many stories of people who claim to be Christians or who in some way carry the label of Christ in religious affiliation, but who live and act in a way that causes people to question that label. These stories are enough to make anyone cringe at the idea of being associated with them. The words "Christian" and "hypocrite" far too often appear in the same sentence when it comes to society's evaluation or critique of the religious. 84% of young adults who would identify themselves as external to the Christian faith say that they personally know at least one Christian; however, only 15% say the lives of the Christians they know are any different from others in society.[1] The chasm between these two numbers is an indictment upon the North American Church, debilitating us from representing Christ and diluting our capacity to affect change. However, the gap in these numbers also positions those who are truly passionate about mirroring Christ to radically stand out against both the godlessly self-centered and the godlessly religious of our society.

Mainstream Western culture is permeated by the sarcastic and overly critical self-righteousness of our generation and therefore exacerbates this commentary on the Church. The Judeo-Christian religious institution is the persistent target of mainstream culture. While Christians are often unfairly expected to be perfect, our failures have sadly earned for us this badge of dishonor, and our reputation or false pretense has deeply affected the Church's potential for credibility or impact.

Although there are many reasons for our diminishing effectiveness, our current condition has largely been borne out of a fundamentally flawed understanding of what it means to be a Christian. When "born-again" Christians were asked, "What would you say are the two or three most important priorities for the Christian to pursue in terms of their faith?" the following picture of "Christianity" emerged.[2]

Top Priorities "Born-Again Christians" Identified in Living out Their Faith	
1 Lifestyle – doing the right thing, being good, not sinning	37%
2 Discipleship – learning about Christ, learning about the Bible	31%
3 Evangelism – explaining/sharing your faith, leading people to Christ	25%
4 Worship – worshiping God, singing	25%
5 Relationships – loving others, making and keeping friends	23%
6 Service – helping others, helping the poor, serving people	18%
7 Stewardship – giving money, time or resources to others	4%
8 Family Faith – discipling your children, shaping family faith	1%
9 Other	2%
10 Not sure	10%

Even by the narrowest definition of Christianity, most people think that the highest priority of being a Christian is to not sin, that to be good and not do "bad" is the highest goal of being a Christian. If we have communicated this picture of what it means to be a Christian, we have also set up the daunting standard by which the world will evaluate us. Most religious insiders primarily define following Christ as a prescribed set of mostly "don'ts." Out of a commendable effort to live "right" and live in a way that distinguishes us from the "world", we have created extra-biblical codes of behavior. As with many evangelical Christians, I grew up with a pretty clear understanding of what Christians shouldn't do for which I later couldn't find biblical support. Far more emotional and spiritual energy is spent trying not to sin or trying to conform to a legalistic, artificial code of behavior than is spent fostering a greater intimacy with Christ that results in a natural, Christ-like lifestyle. Instead of trying to get people not to sin, we should instead be focused on nurturing an environment where people are consumed with, and transformed by, His presence; the right lifestyle will be an inevitable byproduct.

In the most current and extensive research by the Barna Group, David Kinnaman demonstrates in his book, *unChristian*, that over the past decade the "outsiders" perception of Christianity has significantly worsened. In fact, North American society's view of Christianity has never been more negative and un-Christ like. Listen to the findings:

> In our national surveys we found the three most common perceptions of present-day Christianity are antihomosexual (an image held by 91% of young outsiders), judgmental (87%), and hypocritical (85%). These "big three" are followed by the following negative perceptions, embraced by a majority of young adults: old-fashioned, too involved in politics, out of touch with reality, insensitive to others, boring, not accepting of other faiths, and confusing. When they think of the Christian faith, these are the images that come to mind. This is what a new generation really thinks about Christianity.[3]

Two very well-known thinkers and leaders, one a Christ-follower and one not, are often quoted to highlight the reality of our weakened standing in the world. Brennan Manning, a former Catholic priest and popular writer and speaker once said, "The greatest single cause of atheism in the world today is Christians, who acknowledge Jesus with their lips, then walk out the door, and deny Him by their lifestyle. That is what an unbelieving world simply finds unbelievable." Similarly, Mahatma Gandhi is often quoted as having said, "I like your Christ. I do not like your Christians. Your Christians are so unlike your Christ. The materialism of the affluent Christian countries appears to contradict the claims of Jesus Christ." Spoken years apart, from opposite sides of the world, and in difference contexts, these two statements unfortunately capture the candid snapshot that portrays the reality of an ineffectual Church. The dilapidated state of Christianity has reduced it to being considered simply another major world religion, the religion of the West. To most of the world, Christianity is just another option among many belief systems; instead, it should be recognized as the powerful, organic movement that couldn't help but produce a new social reality defined by justice, starting with the world's poor and marginalized, as we read about in the Bible. The biblical picture of a faith that was assumed to be evidenced in how the poor are treated is vastly different from what exists today. What began as the force of power, service, love, and compassion slowly morphed into an institutional and hierarchical religion that has very little resemblance to its original form or Founder. We see in Scripture that it was the sinful and the sick who flocked to Jesus and felt safe in His presence. The same cannot be said of the Church today. The sinful and the sick today generally don't consider the Church a place of grace and emotional safety. The kind of people who hung out with Jesus wouldn't feel welcome in most of our churches.

Off to a Great Start

Most of church history doesn't do us any favors either. Arguably, the most attractive and powerful the Church has ever been was from the time of Acts 2 until the marriage of Church and State by Emperor Constantine in 325. During this time, Christianity was essentially illegal and followers of Christ were persecuted heavily.[4] Refusing to worship the Emperors from the time of Nero until 312, Christians were fed to lions, used as fuel for torches, forced to fight in gladiator games for public entertainment, mutilated, and starved, and their homes and holy books were torched.[5] As God's people expressed during all other times of great persecution, their faith and commitment to God was immovable. The community of believers was strong and their passion for compassion attracted those around them. The following is a quote from an advisor to the Roman Emperor in 137 AD. While he was not a Christian, his words powerfully indicate that he was impacted by what he saw of Christians around him. These words also cause my heart to leap at the possibility that this could be said of the Church again:

> It is the Christians, O Emperor, Who have sought and found the truth, for they acknowledge God. They do not keep for themselves the goods entrusted to them. They do not covet what belongs to others. They show love to their neighbours. They do not do to another what they would not wish to have done to themselves. They speak gently to those who oppress them, and in this way they make them their friends. It has become their passion to do good to their enemies. They live in the awareness of their smallness. Anyone of them who has anything gives ungrudgingly to the one who has nothing. If they see a travelling stranger, they bring him under their roof. They rejoice over him as a real brother, for they do not call one another brothers out of the flesh, but they know that they are brothers in the spirit and in God. If they hear that one of them is imprisoned or oppressed for the sake of Christ, they take care of all his needs. If possible, they set him free. If anyone among them is poor or comes into want while they themselves have nothing to spare, they fast two or three days for him. In this way they can supply any poor man with the food he needs. This O Emperor, is the rule of life of the Christians, and this is their manner of life.[6]

Despite this 300 year period being perhaps the greatest time of persecution of Christians in the last 2000 years, various historians indicate that the Church experienced phenomenal growth. Based on an estimated population of 60 million in the Roman Empire, historians believe that the Church grew from about 1000 people in the year 40 to more than 6 million people by the year 300.[7] How is it that, during a time when becoming a follower of Christ was so dangerously unpopular, the Church actually grew exponentially? In contrast, today, when it has never been easier in some respects to be a Christian, why are people constantly leaving the institutional Church, finding little to no value in religion? Without taking away from the role of the Holy Spirit in conversion growth of the early church, the spiritual climate that existed produced a social reality that was attractive to those on the outside looking in. Rodney Stark makes the following comment about why Christianity was so attractive during its infancy:

> Christian values of love and charity had, from the beginning, been translated into norms of social service and community solidarity. When disaster struck, the Christians were better able to cope, and this resulted in substantially higher rates of survival. This means that in the aftermath of each epidemic, Christians made up a larger percentage of the population even without converts. Moreover, their noticeably better survival rate

would have seemed a miracle to Christians and pagans alike, and this would have influenced conversion.[8]

History Doesn't Help

While I'm sure that the end of persecution was a welcome relief to the early believers, it was the beginning of the spiritual stagnation and institutionalization of the early church. From that point on, the leaders of the Church moved from a dependence on the Holy Spirit and interdependence on the community of faith, to the power and position that came from a new political posture. The marriage of Church and State moved the Church away from a powerful grassroots movement of love and compassion, and into a religious and political institution from which it has never fully recovered. To this day, it is widely acknowledged that the Church of Christ is most powerful and effective when it faces obstacles that force it into a position of dependence on God.

Over the past 1700 years or so, critics of the Church can easily point to times in our history that contradict our message and example of love. Where the Church has become spiritually stagnant and bankrupt, moral decay, social neglect, and even oppression ensue. The Scriptures teach, and history confirms, that social action, or inaction, is a clear barometer of the spiritual health of the community of God.

Some of the world's most gruesome atrocities have been carried out and justified by the world's great religions, Christianity included, leaving little doubt that Christians are no different from followers of other faith systems. Short-sightedness might cause us to look at the past couple of decades and abhor the incredibly dark actions of Hindu and Muslim extremists against each other and against Christians in places like India, Pakistan, Indonesia, Iraq, Afghanistan, and of course in the U.S. on 9/11. However, those with a little more historical awareness would be just as correct in pointing out the equally dark history of Christianity. They could point to the Crusades where Christians thought that the best way to "re-Christianize" the Holy Land was to force out, brutalize, and kill the Arabs and Muslims who lived there. They could remind us of the Catholic Church's attempt, throughout history, to force people to recant heresy by torture or be burned at the stake. They could talk about the fact that, for years, Protestant and Catholic violence in Northern Ireland resulted in hatred and bloodshed of fellow Irishmen. The current atrocities by religious extremists which the media pipes into our homes don't hold a candle to some of the violence and brutality carried out in the name of Jesus Christ over history. I wonder what will be said about us when the history books are written about Christians or church history in the twentieth century. I wonder if it will be argued that our lack of action on the current issues of global imbalance, poverty, and preventable suffering will be viewed as an ignorant, passive brutality on par with and maybe with an even greater death toll than any of the past, more intentional, acts of violence attributed to the Church.

A couple of years ago, I was having a conversation with an irreligious friend of mine about religion. After hearing about his encounters with Christianity in his past, it is no wonder he could be the "poster-boy" for what much of the secular world thinks about Christians. In our conversation he said, "I don't have a problem if people are religious but what I can't stand is people who are extreme in their religion." As I thought about the current events that informed the perspective he expressed in that comment, I paused for a second to think about how to respond. And then it struck me: "When people think about those who are extreme in their religious commitment," I said, "we tend to think about them as close minded, arrogant, forceful, and judgmental toward those who are not part of their religion. However," I continued, "that is the opposite of Who Jesus was and how He acted. Jesus was compassionate to the sinner, He fed the hungry, healed the sick, cared for children, and exuded a love and compassion that drew thousands to follow. He also opposed the religious establishment of His day. So, really, the problem is that we are not extreme enough. If we were simply extremely like Jesus we would then demonstrate the antithesis of what you hate about those who are religious extremists."

The thought I was trying to express to my friend is so well put by Bruxy Cavey in his book, *The End of Religion*:

The problem with many 'Christian fundamentalists' is that they are not fundamental enough. Please understand whenever the Christian Church has become violent or intolerant, or just plain uncharitable, it is not because of a fundamentalist adherence to the teachings of Jesus but precisely the opposite. It is because his teachings have been patently ignored and replaced with the prevailing ethos of the day, masquerading as religious dogma.[9]

Although my friend was caused to think about his perspective a little more, I still felt my words were being met with a whole torrent of history and life experience that had convinced him of the opposite. I felt as if my words were as effective as trying to swim up Niagara Falls.

As we examined previously in Part One, it is obvious that mainstream Christianity in North America is starved for the power and presence of Jesus. Without it, we are left with an empty religious façade that is not only useless to affect global change but it also actually contributes to the creation of agnostics and atheists. David Kinnaman writes:

Young outsiders and Christians alike do not want a cheap, ordinary, or insignificant life, but their vision of present-day Christianity is just that – superficial, antagonistic, and depressing. The Christian life looks so simplified and constricted that a new generation no longer recognizes it as a sophisticated, livable response to a complex world.[10]

So much needs to change. With the picture of what *is* so painfully imbedded in our minds, I want to allow the Word of God to paint us a new old picture of what *can be*. Then, we will look at the transformation that must occur if we are to re-claim and re-live the biblical picture of a powerfully compassionate Church that can change the world and, in doing so, point the spotlight squarely on our Master and Friend.

Chapter 4 - So now what?

1. Think about some of the people you interact with who don't follow Christ. What is it that some of them have said or would say about Christianity?

2. Would you agree that "Christians are a bunch of hypocrites"? Why or why not?

3. What would an extreme follower of Christ look like?

4. What impacted you about any of the stories from Chapter 4?

5. What would you say should be the most important qualities of a believer?

6. From your experiences, describe some of the qualities of a church you see as spiritually bankrupt and some of the qualities of a church you feel is functioning the way it was intended.

7. What is it that causes many outsiders to see Christianity as anti-homosexual, judgmental, and/or hypocritical?

8. Identify an experience where someone you know (or know of) was positively impacted by a follower of Christ.

Chapter 5

The Old Testament Picture

In the Old Testament, we witness God interacting with His people for hundreds of years and a clear picture develops of God's intent and design for abundant spiritual health that is manifested in social systems and realities. Just as relevant as the message is today, God draws unambiguous differences between auto-pilot religious activity and authentic spiritual vibrancy. In this chapter we will start to see a clear picture between the spiritual health of God's people and the social health of the poor.

Before we look at the words of the prophets, let's understand the general context of these messages. It is crucial to note that while God's anger and message focused heavily on social injustice, this was symptomatic of the core disease afflicting His people; idolatry was the root spiritual problem that evidenced itself in social sin. When God's people lost their first love, they failed to tangibly love those in need around them. God constantly points to social injustice as evidence of misplaced spiritual affection.

To avoid the common pitfalls of building a theology and practice around the dangerous habit of proof texting, let's examine several snapshots taken over generations. This unfortunately common practice of proof texting sees people use the Bible to back their predetermined hypotheses and conclusions, often by taking passages out of context. Pet issues and soap boxes are often supported by isolated references, ignoring vital contextual information that would aid in proper interpretation. Before we look to various passages from Scripture to form our vision of a compassionate Church, we first need to recognize that some of what we will read is descriptive (describing what is happening in a specific situation), some is prescriptive (providing specific instructions or imperatives), and some is both. There are windows into situations where compassion, or the lack of it, is portrayed by the writer as the consequences of whatever spiritual climate is being described. However, the lifestyle of compassion and generosity is prescribed throughout Scripture as both an end and a means to an end. It is prescribed as the result, or outflow, of healthy spirituality, and often presented as the means to experience the power and presence of God in our lives.

The following list of Scripture passages related to poverty and compassion is by no means exhaustive. The themes of poverty, compassion, justice, money, wealth, possessions, and greed are woven throughout the writing of Scripture over thousands of years. Those I reference in the pages that follow only scratch the surface of the relevant topics. I would suggest you take the time to read each biblical text or chapter noted before proceeding with my words.

> *Isaiah 1 – "Wash yourselves and be clean! Get your sins out of my sight. Give up your evil ways. Learn to do good. Seek justice. Help the oppressed. Defend the cause of orphans. Fight for the rights of widows"* (Isaiah 1:16-17).

This opening chapter of Isaiah's book doesn't ease into the issue very gently at all. God is ticked off. As fits the job description of a prophet, Isaiah is given a message of warning by God. Prophets knew the times they were in and knew what God was saying in those times; as a result, they were not so popular. They called for repentance and transformation and warned of the consequences of not changing. This first chapter of Isaiah sets the tone for the message of the book.

God is bringing an indictment against His people: they had replaced spiritual substance with religious form. He starts by showing the pain of a father's heart. He has nurtured and raised His children; however, even farm animals were better at obeying their master than His own children (vs. 2-4). After pointing out the symptoms of their sin and the consequence of rebellion (vs. 5-9), God addresses the leaders and the followers, specifically condemning the conduct of the religious activity He previously instructed them to engage in (vs. 10-15). It is amazing to hear God say things like, *"What makes you think I want all of your sacrifices?...I am sick of your burnt offerings...Who asked you to worship me with all your ceremony?...I want no more of your pious meetings...I hate your celebrations and your annual festivals...I cannot stand them...When you lift up your hands in prayer, I will not look. Though you offer many prayers, I will not listen"* (Isaiah 1:11-15).

Wow! That would be like God walking into one of our big churches, interrupting the service, and saying, "Why are you doing all of this? It's all meaningless and a waste of time. I'm sick and tired of your Sunday morning services and your worship teams; it's all just annoying noise to me! I hate your mid-week programs and annual church retreats. Oh, and by the way, I've completely tuned out your Wednesday night prayer meetings, so don't bother coming out!"

In these five verses, God totally dismantles the core religious systems that have come to represent His presence on the earth among His people. Then He calls them to repentance, essentially equating their religious activity with sin itself. He calls them to change and to refocus on activity that authenticates their relationship with Him. And then, here it is. He is looking for the evidence of true relationship: *"Do good. Seek justice. Help the oppressed. Defend the cause of orphans. Fight for the rights of widows"* (Isaiah 1:17). That's it? That's it.

God links spiritual condition to social priorities. He draws the direct line between a right relationship with Him and their right relationship with the poor and defenseless. It is not their adherence to religious forms and systems that acts as a spiritual heart monitor: it is what they do for the lonely and oppressed.

Isaiah 58 – "Feed the hungry, and help those in trouble. Then your light will shine out from the darkness and the darkness around you will be as bright as noon. The Lord will guide you continually, giving you water when you are dry and restoring your strength" (Isaiah 58:10-11).

More than anything else I read in the Old Testament, Isaiah 58 marries spirituality to social justice. Again, God is brazenly upset with His people, so much so that He wants this message shouted with a trumpet blast to get their attention (vs. 1). This is not the "still, small voice" of God. This is the "red faced, get your attention" voice of God. The chapter heading in my Bible labels this chapter as "True and False Worship". The chapter heading in the NIV translation labels this chapter as "True Fasting." and in the Message version says, "Your Prayers Won't Get Off The Ground."

God starts this memo by telling the prophet to yet again point out the sins of His people. Verse 2 levels the accusation, *"They act* so pious! They come to the Temple every day and seem delighted to learn all about me. They act like a righteous nation that would never abandon the laws of God. They ask me to take action on their behalf, pretending they want to be near me"* (Isaiah 58:2).

Ouch! Hear the words again, "Act...seem...act...pretend." God's anger is evoked with the religious pretense again. He is more than miffed that His relationship with His people comes down to nothing more than religious theater.

The first part of verse 3 gives us some indication that at least they recognize that something isn't right in their relationship with God, despite the fact that they thought they were doing alright in the religion department. *"'We have fasted before you!' they say. 'Why aren't you impressed? We have been very hard on ourselves, and you don't even notice it'"* (Isaiah 58:3).

Things aren't adding up. They are being ultra-religious and God is still silent. They are even fasting and subjecting themselves to extreme self-denial in order to gain an audience and employ the favor of God. They are going to pious extremes and still God isn't taking notice of them. How much more religious could they be? It appears that God's silence and absence indicates to them that something significant is missing from their spirituality. It seems like they desire God's presence and that this void is causing them to realize that there is something more that they are missing.

Then, as if God had already prepared His closing arguments on His case, He opens fire. "I'll tell you why!" He responds. God then seems to transition from a discussion about religious practices to a tirade about how His people are treating those around them. He brings up the fact that while they were fasting they were also oppressing their workers and arguing with each other. Then He says, *"This kind of fasting will never get you anywhere with me"* (Isaiah 58:4).

It is powerful and poignant that God uses the ascetic spiritual discipline of fasting to paint the picture of their spiritual emptiness. The spiritual value of fasting is clearly seen throughout Scripture, and modeled by Christ, as a way to usher God's power and presence into the lives of His people. Yet here God harshly criticizes His people for thinking physical fasting is all that's needed to engage His activity in their lives. *"You humble yourself by going through the motions of penance, bowing your heads like reeds bending in the wind. You dress yourself in burlap and cover yourself with ashes. Is this what you call fasting? Do you really think this will please the Lord?"* (Isaiah 58:5).

If I were being asked these questions, my immediate answer would be, "Yes…I actually did think that this kind of fasting would please You and cause You to listen to me when I pray and act on my behalf when I needed You!" However, in the very next verse, God answers His own questions with a big, "No!"

Despite the fact that we have a record of this dialogue between God and His people from thousands of years ago, we do exactly the same thing today. Woven into the fabric of religious culture is the assumption that the more committed we are to the faithful adherence to whatever traditions have become sacred, the more pleased God will be with us. Consequently, the more pleased He is with us the more entitled we feel to His positive actions on our behalf. We try to earn His favor and support by the degree of our devotion.

Next, God redefines worship and fasting, and even the concept of religion itself. It is what God says next that has me absolutely convinced the world would be transformed if only we would take it seriously: *"This is the kind of fasting I want. Free those who are imprisoned; lighten the burden of those who work for you. Let the oppressed go free, and remove the chains that bind people. Share your food with the hungry, and give shelter to the homeless. Give clothes to those who need them, and do not hide from relatives who need your help"* (Isaiah 58:6-7).

Incredible! God marries the concept of extreme spiritual discipline with a radical selfless outward focus on the world. Again, the test of our spiritual temperature is tied directly to what we do about and for the needs of those around us, not to our strict adherence to spiritual disciplines alone.

Another thing I love about Isaiah 58 is how it promises the immediate spiritual return on social investment. Remember the beginning of the chapter? God's people are confused and frustrated by God's silence and inactivity despite their impeccable religious checklist. The chapter ends with an incredibly attractive description of what God promises to those who will *"feed the hungry and help those in trouble."* God says that if you do these things, *"Then your salvation will come...your wounds will quickly heal...your godliness will lead you forward...the glory of the Lord will protect you...you will call and the Lord will quickly reply, 'Yes. I am here'...your light will shine out from the darkness...the Lord will guide you continually...he will give you water when you are dry... and restore your strength...you will be like a well watered garden, like an ever flowing spring...some of you will rebuild the deserted ruins of your cities"* (Isaiah 58:8-12).

God is quick to respond to His people when His people respond to the needs of those suffering around them. Likewise, His power and presence in our lives, individually and corporately, are directly proportional to, and conditional on, what we do or don't do for the hungry, the sick, the lonely, the burdened, the oppressed, or those who just need our help. There is a plain and consistent message that God is saying to His people: "If you want me to pay attention to you, then you pay attention to the poor."

Jeremiah 5 & 22 – "Among my people are wicked men... they are fat and sleek and there is no limit to their wicked deeds. They refuse to provide justice to orphans and deny the rights of the poor"... "[Josiah] gave justice and help to the poor and needy and everything went well for him. Isn't that what it means to know me?', says the Lord" (Jeremiah 5:26-28 and 22:16).

Jeremiah is another prophet whose job it was to warn and instruct God's people to turn and head in the opposite direction. Known as the weeping prophet, Jeremiah watched in sadness as God's people suffered the monumental and devastating consequences of refusing to change. When they ignored all the warnings, God used the pagan nation Babylon to humble and discipline His people; the Israel nation and Jerusalem were destroyed and the surviving people and possessions were taken into exile to serve the Babylonian Empire. To get a sense of the humiliation and destruction that God brought upon His people, read the book of Lamentations, which was also written by Jeremiah. God told Jeremiah from the start of his mandate that while he was to preach and warn the nation, they would not listen (vs. 5-19). I can't imagine how difficult it would be as a preacher to have God tell you right up front, "Here is what I want you to preach, but I can tell you right now, no one is going to listen. Preach it anyway."

Like Isaiah, whose message was separated from Jeremiah's by more than a century, Jeremiah lays out the indictment against the people of God. He shows them the symptoms of their spiritual terminal illness. And like Isaiah, Jeremiah points to the social effects of their spiritual poverty. From the second to fifth chapter, God presents His case against His people. In the face of all that God had done for them throughout history, He charges them with abandonment: worshiping idols and pledging allegiance to false gods. He compares them to an adulterous wife who cheats on her faultless husband, and likens them to prodigal children who walk away from a perfect father. To all the evidence of spiritual bankruptcy, God adds this accusation to the list of offences: *"My people have stubborn and rebellious hearts. They have turned away and abandoned me. Like a cage filled with birds, their homes are filled with evil plots. And now they are great and rich. They are fat and sleek, and there is no limit to their wicked deeds. They refuse to provide justice to orphans and deny the rights of the poor"* (Jeremiah 5:23, 27-28).

Here again, God looks at the imbalance of resources as a characteristic of spiritual depravity. Could God not say the same about us today? As I said earlier, in light of the fact that "Christian" nations, 20% of the world population, are fat and living on more than 80% of the world's resources while more than half of the world population lives in dire poverty, couldn't the very same indictment be brought against us?

Comparing the wickedness of King Jehoiakim to the righteousness of his father King Josiah, God gives the son reasons why his father had been blessed and enjoyed God's favor. Jehoiakim's priority was to enjoy the extravagant life that came from a sense of entitlement, enabled by great resources and power. In contrast, Josiah had also enjoyed the blessings of abundance, but never overlooked the poor. Speaking through Jeremiah, God points out the difference to Jehoiakim: *"a beautiful palace does not make a great King. Your father, Josiah, also had plenty to eat and drink. But he was just and right in all his dealings. That is why God blessed him. He gave justice and help to the poor and needy, and everything went well for him. Isn't this what it means to know me?"* (Jeremiah 22:15-16).

It's important to note here that God doesn't condemn wealth. In fact, He blesses people with great wealth. Over the years, many anti-poverty advocates or spiritual leaders have come out against wealth, equating the possession, or even the enjoyment, of wealth as sinful. Like many other examples in Scripture, Jeremiah points out that it's what we do with wealth and our priorities that either bring God's further blessing or bring His condemnation. Josiah had plenty, and he used what he had for the poor and needy. Jehoiakim also had plenty, but he spent it on himself.

Here again God is equating what is done for the poor and needy with the very essence of true spirituality. *"He [Josiah] gave justice and help to the poor and needy…isn't this what it means to know me?"* (Jeremiah 22:16).

For those who have any desire to know God more, this one verse holds great importance. This concept of worship through compassion is fairly uncommon in the current evangelical climate. In an effort to move away from liberation theology and the social gospel, to focus less on the immediate and temporal, the evangelical have swung the pendulum to the opposite and out-of-touch extreme. Our evangelistic zeal has relegated compassion and social conscience to an optional afterthought of outreach and mission. A theology and practice of evangelism without social justice ignores a valid function of ministry, and even more so, it diminishes an essential component of healthy personal and corporate spirituality. Many times, I have heard from evangelical Christian leaders and organizations, "We need to give them a Bible, not a loaf of bread. We need to focus on getting them into Heaven. That's where they will spend eternity. The priority for our time and treasure needs to be evangelism rather than relief and development."

Without for a moment disparaging the value of proclaiming God's good news in the person of Jesus and His work on the cross, the idea that social justice or practical provision for the poor is an optional side activity for those who are "called" to that type of thing has us squarely caught in social sin referred to many times as evil. The words of the ancient prophets to the nation of Israel are just as pertinent to the body of Christ in the Western world today. By not actively and purposefully providing for the world's poor and needy out of our extreme abundance, we have, according to Jeremiah, also forgotten what it means to truly know God.

For those who are hungry for spiritual life, hungry to know the power and presence of God, for those who are desperate for the life of God to fill the Western Church again, we must take bold leadership and move into a world that is hungry for physical life and do something about it.

> *Ezekiel 18 – "He gives food to the hungry and provides clothes for the needy. He helps the poor, does not lend money at interest, and obeys all my regulations and decrees. Such a person will not die because of his father's sins; he will surely live"* (Ezekiel 18:16-17).

Ezekiel was the next major prophet to come after Jeremiah. He was one of the few to survive the fall of Jerusalem and was taken into the Babylonian captivity. Ezekiel was used by God to speak to the remnant of His people in Babylon. In the early years of the captivity of God's people, very little had changed regarding the very spiritual condition that led to the destruction of Jerusalem.[1] Much of what Isaiah and Jeremiah had preached was still being spoken by Ezekiel. Even after their humiliation and destruction the Israelites still didn't understand what was wrong with their relationship with God. God was using Ezekiel to drive home the painful lessons of sin and set the stage for God's plan to restore the relationship again with His people.

In the first half of his book, Ezekiel describes the sin of God's people in a way very similar to the words of Jeremiah. He compares the lives of Josiah and Jehoiakim to draw direct links to the differences between how God's people *should* be living and how they *have been* living. Ezekiel talks about a wicked man (vs. 10-

13) who demonstrates his sinful condition by worshiping idols, committing adultery, oppressing the poor and helpless, lending money at excessive interest rates, and committing detestable acts. There it is again: God lumps ignoring the poor and needy right up there with worshiping idols and adultery. God then talks about this man's son (vs. 14-17) who sees the father's sinful life and decides he will have none of that. He refuses to worship idols and commit adultery. He doesn't take advantage of the poor, but instead gives them food and clothing.

The main point of this chapter in Ezekiel isn't to establish a comprehensive theology of social justice as an extension of healthy spirituality but rather to contrast a wicked, sinful person that elicits God's judgment against a righteous person who is experiencing real life. Beyond the comparison, however, we need to realize that it's not an option to live a life with a priority and value for extending the practical demonstration of God's love to the poor: a person or a gathering of God's people or even a nation that doesn't have as part of its very culture an active, visible manifestation of care, can very well anticipate either God's absence or eventually the rod of God's judgment.

The Western Church is far from living a culture of compassion, and we are in line for the same messages that ring from Isaiah, Jeremiah, and Ezekiel. While warm pockets of compassion do exist within the Church, the global imbalance of resources tells us that it is not enough to think that token giving to the benevolent fund or emergency appeals will restore God's favor and power upon His people.

> *Amos – "Listen to me, you fat cows living in Samaria, you women who oppress the poor and crush the needy, and who are always calling to your husbands, "Bring us another drink!" For I know the vast number of your sins and the depth of your rebellions. You oppress good people by taking bribes and deprive the poor of justice in the courts. Hate what is evil and love what is good; turn your courts into true halls of justice. Perhaps even yet the Lord God of Heaven's Armies will have mercy on the remnant of his people"* (Amos 4:1; 5:12,15).

Amos preached at about the same time as Isaiah, when God's people were powerful and prosperous. Life was so good that they compared this time in history to the reign of King David. They were safe and secure from foreign threats and exceedingly comfortable with the extent of their wealth.[2] As we know too well, this description of Israel's wealth was a barometer of their spiritual poverty. Echoing the messages of the Major Prophets, Israel and Judah's political and spiritual leaders had taken their nations into idolatry and worship of Baal.

Amos hammers together the social and spiritual realities. In the beginning of the book the prophet puts forward a description of Israel's sin. In the same thought, God puts the mistreatment of the poor on the same plane as the evil of incest: *"They trample helpless people in the dust and shove the oppressed out of the way. Both father and son sleep with the same woman, corrupting my holy name"* (Amos 2:7).

Stop and think about that: with the same breath, God equates the severity and consequences of incest and sexual debauchery with the way His people treated the poor!

Bringing a magnifying glass to their sin issue, Amos also goes further into the fabric of society than the other Major Prophets. In a number of verses throughout the book, he uses the word "trample" when it comes to describing the social sin (2:7, 5:11, 8:4), revealing that the social evil to which he is referring is economic injustice that keeps the poor under the feet of the wealthy. He condemns their economic systems that continue to benefit the rich, and he uses harsh words like trample, steal and rob: *"You trample the poor, stealing their grain through taxes and unfair rent. Therefore, though you build beautiful stone houses, you will never live in them. Though you plant lush vineyards, you will never drink wine from them...and* [you] *deprive the poor of justice in your courts"* (Amos 5:10-12).

It is far beyond the scope of this book to uncover all the ways Western nations today are guilty of sinful economic injustice in dealings with developing countries. God's people today, unknowingly for the most part, are supporting the unjust economic systems that allow us to stay comfortable at the expense of 80% of the world's population. From trade policy to debt payments, from the lack of adequate development assistance to the prevalence of economically-driven foreign policy, we are trampling the world's poor. The problem with the unjust social structures and financial systems is that we are veiled to its effects on the developing world. The media regularly broadcasts the violence of terror attacks but the carnage of inequity and injustice claims far more lives on a daily basis. Our full participation in the economic engine of consumerism not only accounts for more money than the average person earns in North America, but it also continues to subjugate the poor in developing nations. Frankly, we are guilty by association and compliance.

I am not an economist (my wife looks after our family finances!), nor am I an expert on the policies of international trade and globalization; however, I can tell you that while international trade and a globalized economy have benefited a few countries, these same policies have further trampled the poorest of the poor. I have been to India and China in the past few years and have seen some of the positive effects of globalization. I have also been to Haiti and Kenya and have witnessed substantially more people who are unable to buy rice to feed their children because of the negative effects. In Vince Gallagher's book, *The True Cost of Low Prices*, the author brings light to the negative effects of globalization and unjust economic priorities:

The reason so many people are dying of hunger is not because there isn't enough food. Virtually every "hungry" country produces enough food for all of its people. The essential problem is the food is not distributed fairly. Distribution is regulated by political and economic decision makers, and rarely by the people themselves. It is the powerful who decide who has access to an abundant food supply and who does not. There is enough wheat, rice, and other grains produced to feed every person with 3,600 calories a day – much more than we need. The reality is that many poor countries export more food than they import.[3]

According to Amos and confirmed by our current global economic situation, God's people had better focus our heads and priorities beyond our own comfort and truly try to understand and affect change on the sinful systems to which we contribute at the expense of the poor. The message of Amos to the nations of Israel and Judah is as urgent today as it was then: we have become addicted to our comforts and obsessed with feeding our already overstuffed lifestyles (like fat cows), while we turn our backs on the painful daily realities of more than a billion starving neighbors. Yet again, we have another prophet telling us that there is an intimate connection between our relationship with God and our relationship with the poor.

Micah 6 – "What can we bring to the Lord? What kind of offerings should we give him? Should we bow before God with offerings of yearling calves? Should we offer him thousands of rams and ten thousand rivers of olive oil? Should we sacrifice our firstborn children to pay for our sins? No, O people, the Lord has told you what is good, and this is what he requires of you: to do what is right, to love mercy, and to walk humbly with your God" (Micah 6:6-8).

Micah was a contemporary of Isaiah and preaches into the same context of spiritual and social depravity. A major focus for Micah is his direct aim at the religious and political leaders of God's people. He holds them responsible for the bankrupt spiritual condition and the social injustice that resulted. He accuses the religious leaders of supporting the unjust systems and practices that *"steal the shirts right off of the backs of those who trusted you, evicting women from the pleasant homes and forever stripping their children of all that God would give them"* (Micah 2:8-9).

Micah 6:8 is famous. Worship songs have been written with these words and many could quote this passage from memory. However, this verse is made even more poignant by the questions that come before it, which reveal an amazingly simple, yet crystal clear, picture that summarizes what the prophets had been trying to say for hundreds of years. This verse also could act as the mission statement for any church or individual today that wants to simplify everything to the basics of the Christian faith.

The beginning of Chapter 6 starts with God bringing His case against His people again. He reminds them of His past faithfulness and nurture. He reminds them of how He cared for them from the time He delivered them from Egypt, and recalls the stories of their ancestors, retracing the evidence of His love and faithfulness.

Then His people respond by asking, "What is it that you want from us?!" This is more of a devotional thought than an attempt at correct interpretation, but I read these questions from God's people as an exasperated challenge to God. I see them throwing up their hands and saying, "Look! What is it that you want from us anyway!?" Then they start with a question that assumes God is looking for devotion through adherence to religious systems. They ask what type of offering they should bring before Him. Then they quickly get downright ridiculous in their inquiry. "What is it that's going to get you off our backs? Do you want offerings of young calves? No? Then how about 1000 rams? Still not enough? Then how about 10,000 rivers of olive oil? (As if there was such a thing.) Still not happy, God? Then why don't we sacrifice our first-born child, like the pagans do for their gods? Is that what it's going to take to pay for our rebellion?"

"No. None of that," replies God. "I've already told you what I want from you. And here it is: To do what is right, to love mercy, and to walk humbly with me." It's just that simple. In all of the complexities and messed up systems of religion, trying to figure out how we are to live as the people of God, it comes down to such a simple purpose that is often difficult to live. Hear it again: To act with justice, to love mercy, and to walk humbly with God. Sounds an awful lot like the simplicity of Isaiah 1:17: "*Learn to do good. Seek justice. Help the oppressed. Defend the cause of orphans. Fight for the rights of widows.*"

Consistent with the message of the prophets is this core idea that our relationship with God will be manifested in whatever we do or don't do for those in need.

> *Zechariah 7 – "And even now in your holy festivals, aren't you eating and drinking just to please yourselves? Isn't this the same message the Lord proclaimed through the prophets in years past...? This is what the Lord of Heaven's Armies says: Judge fairly, and show mercy and kindness to one another. Do not oppress widows, orphans, foreigners, and the poor... And do not scheme against each other. Your ancestors refused to listen to this message. They stubbornly turned away and put their fingers in their ears to keep from hearing...They made their hearts as hard as stone, so they could not hear the instructions or the messages that the Lord of Heaven's Armies had sent them by his Spirit through the earlier prophets. That is why the Lord of Heaven's Armies was so angry with them"* (Zechariah 7:6-7, 9-12).

Zechariah was born while the Jews were captive in Babylon and takes his place as God's mouthpiece as He prepares His people for repatriation.[4] His job is to prepare the hearts and spirits of God's people for the promise of returning to Jerusalem to start all over. The prophet is bringing the message of hope and encouragement that the prison sentence they had endured for 70 years was soon to be over and the remnant would return to rebuild God's nation.

However, God is starting to get a little concerned about what He is seeing start to crop up with His remnant. Creeping back into the life of His people is the shadow of what got them into this situation in the first place. Even after all of the "in-your-face" warnings, even after all of the pain and suffering and destruction of the exile, God's people are starting to slip back into their old ways of forgetting about the poor while they enjoy themselves. God is preparing His people to return to Jerusalem for the long awaited restoration after 70 years of being the slaves of a pagan king, punishment for their spiritual and social habitual sin.

Zechariah soon hears from God and is quick to jump all over this burning ember from the past inferno of spiritual and social depravity. Essentially he says, "Now just wait a minute! Do we see what is happening here? It's got a whole lot of similarities to what got us in this mess. Let's remember for a minute what happened to our parents and grandparents and why it happened. When times were prosperous, our ancestors constantly forgot about and even oppressed the poor and apparently the needy have a very special place in God's heart. So, while we enjoy benefits, of His blessing let's be *very* careful never to forget about the orphans, widows, the foreigners, and the poor." Zechariah plays for them a scene from their past to remind them that the hope of their future has to be different. They must build into the DNA of their spirituality a new social reality that reflects the heart of God, or they will again be facing the Lord of Heaven's Armies.

I love the title that Zechariah uses for God a few times here: the Lord of Heaven's Armies. In fact, for a relatively small book, Zechariah uses this name for God 56 times out of the 249 times it's used in the whole of Scripture. We can conclude that this continual reference to the Lord of Heaven's Armies is meant to define who He is to this remnant. He is more powerful than all of the kingdoms of this earth and this has the potential to bring both great comfort and great fear to His people. If the Lord of Heaven's Armies fights for the rights of widows and orphans and the poor, we had better also.

•

For Example

While in Delhi, India in early 2008, I had the privilege of traveling to the south and visiting the ministry of Dr. P.P. Job, who is often referred to as the Billy Graham of India. In addition to his evangelistic work, literature work, education, and medical work, Dr. Job started an orphanage that houses more than 500 girls from babies to college age. These girls are all at the orphanage because their parents were martyred for their faith or they were abandoned by parents who didn't want a girl. Appropriate to his last name, Dr. Job and his wife lost both of their sons to martyrdom when they were killed by religious extremists for preaching the gospel in different parts of Asia. So, needless to say, Dr. Job has a burning passion to assist young girls who have lost their parents in the same way that he lost his sons.

One evening, as we visited with some of the girls, I met Amy. Amy was only a baby when she was brought to the orphanage. She doesn't know anything about her parents or where she came from because when she was only a few weeks old, an old man found her behind a factory. The old man was a night watchman at the factory, and when he heard a small child crying, he searched the grounds with his flashlight and came upon a baby buried up to her neck in the ground. Her mouth was filled with mud, and she was left to die. Her father and mother buried her alive, simply because they didn't want to have a girl. The groundskeeper brought her to the orphanage and she was taken in as one of Dr. Job's children. That evening, I spent time with Amy. She showed me her homework and where she slept and the shelf where she kept all her clothes. She had an electric smile, somehow larger for knowing she had once been buried alive like yesterday's garbage.

Why the story? Because this story, and those in it, illustrates the picture and priorities we read about in the Old Testament passages we just looked at. Over and over again, throughout countless generations, we read that social justice is inextricably linked to our relationship with God. Social sin was not defined as we typically would today: divorce, addictions, broken families, or sexual promiscuity. Social evil was primarily embodied in the effects of a gross imbalance of resources and its consequences on orphans, widows, refugees, and the poor. Spiritual depravity was evidenced in the self-centered failure to pay proper attention to God and the oppressed. On the other hand, spiritual vibrancy was evidenced in the self-emptying priorities of a life that was lived seeking God's face and then reflecting His likeness to those in desperate need.

However, even as I write this, a comprehensive look at the Old Testament vision of spiritual vibrancy and social justice causes deep concern. It doesn't take very long to see the similarities between the state of God's people and the world *then* and the state of God's people and the world *now*. The unprecedented imbalance of resources and economic structures that geographically favors the "Christian West" has us on a collision course with the priorities of God. It's not at all a stretch to say that God's judgment on the Church in North America today is inevitable.

Overlapping the current culture of Christianity with the Old Testament vision of healthy spirituality, it is obvious that the Western Church's concept of spirituality is cut far short in a way which has left us with merely the pretense of religious forms. In our pursuit of effective ministry in the Western Church, we have, by and large, completely ignored the plight of social injustice and the poor. At the risk of sounding repetitive, the Old Testament vision of a right relationship with God combines spiritual renewal with social renovation as two halves of the same body.

As we move now to the New Testament I want us to fix our eyes on Jesus as we look for a biblical vision of a compassionate Church. Looking ahead by several hundred years, the prophet Isaiah sets us up with a job description for the Messiah: *"The Spirit of the Sovereign Lord is upon me, for the Lord has appointed me to bring good news to the poor. He has sent me to comfort the broken hearted and proclaim that captives will be released and prisoners will be freed"* (Isaiah 61:1).

Then one day, hundreds of years later Jesus walks into His home synagogue, gets up, and opens the scroll to Isaiah 61 and reads, *"The Spirit of the Lord is upon me, for he has anointed me to bring Good News to the poor. He has sent me to proclaim that captives will be released, that the blind will see, that the oppressed will be set free"* (Luke 4:18).

Luke tells us that all eyes are "intently" on Him as He rolls up the scroll again and gives it back. Then, breaking the awkward silence, Jesus says, "I'm the One we've all been waiting for."

Chapter 5 - So now what?

1. Which Old Testament passages impacted you the most?

2. What do you see as a consistent thread or principle being taught in these passages of Scripture?

3. Do you think that God makes His power and presence conditional on what we do for the poor? Why or why not?

4. What passage will most likely impact your values or behavior?

5. Why do you think that God seems to have a "soft spot" for the poor?

6. How would you compare the spiritual condition of God's people in the Old Testament with the spiritual condition of churches today?

7. Based on what you read in these passages, what specifically could you or your church change in order to experience spiritual renewal or revival?

Chapter 6

The New Testament Picture

The Old Testament paints us a clear picture of the kind of relationship that God wanted and designed for His people, a relationship that prioritized and exemplified what it looked like for a community to pay attention to God *and* the poor. In the New Testament, we see those values embodied and lived out in the person of Jesus as well as examples of what it looked like for the community of God to embody and live out those same values. This initial blueprint and snapshot of the life and priorities of the earliest days of the Church set the mold for all who would come after. While our look at several Old Testament references takes place over several hundred years and in the context of many different historical, geographical, and political situations, our look at these New Testament players is within the single context of first century Palestine.

As discussed before in our look into the Old Testament, there have been far too many examples of Christian teachers and leaders taking Scripture out of context and isolating one or two passages to build support for a pet issue. With that in mind, we will look at a few different pictures and passages to build our overview of the Word of God.

> *The Life and Words of Jesus - "The Spirit of the Lord is upon me, for he has anointed me to bring Good News to the poor. He has sent me to proclaim that captives will be released, that the blind will see, that the oppressed will be set free"* (Luke 4:18).

God invaded the world in the person of Jesus. He didn't come as they had hoped or as we might expect. You'd think that with the herculean job He had in front of Him, He would have come in a more impressive, advantageous way. You'd think that it would have been more expedient to His mission to come as "The Lord of Heaven's Armies" or the "King of Kings and Lord of Lords." And, while He was certainly all of that, He entered the world He created as a helpless infant born to teenage parents from a low social class. The fact that He arrived in such a lowly manner was another sign that the poor were of special affection. As we have already said, Jesus' job description was written hundreds of years before He reported for duty. With this job description, and against the backdrop of the messages of the prophets, we are also given a comprehensive picture of the priorities of those who would follow Him.

Jesus communicates right off the bat that He isn't there for the religious establishment. If anything, we see built into His mission and message a subversive and often antagonistic posture toward organized religion. The religious institution of the day, propagated by the Pharisees, had long outlived its usefulness and now existed for its own purposes.

The Pharisees were first established when God's people returned to Jerusalem from the exile in Babylon. Their job as religious leaders was to ensure that God's people remained holy and did what God wanted them to do and didn't do what He didn't want. To complicate matters, the people of Israel were not permitted by their former captors to have a King or a political ruler when they returned to Jerusalem, so these religious leaders also became the defacto rulers. Their word and their system became the religious law and civil rule.

The original intent of the Pharisees was bang on – to prioritize, promote, and protect holiness. But after a few hundred years, by the time Christ was on the scene, the same thing had happened as centuries before: the religious institution became the priority in and of itself, rather than the One and the people it was set up to serve. The self-serving religious elite were on par with the self-serving social and political elite. Organized religion was alive and well again, and God and the poor were once again abandoned.

It was into this complicated political and religious climate that Jesus showed up and created major waves. This no-name, illegitimate son of a carpenter with no religious training or pedigree walked right onto the religious center stage and announced that He was the long awaited Messiah and He had come for the poor, the blind, and the oppressed. But then He moved into territory that allowed Him to be known as more than just a social activist: He went about forgiving sins, equating Himself with God, performing miracles, raising the dead, feeding the multitudes with a little boy's lunch, hanging out with thieves and loose women, and consequently attracting huge crowds. Then He got right up in the face of the religious rulers and called them hypocrites, white washed tombs, and a bunch of poisonous snakes, and told them that they were making people twice the sons of Hell than they already were. How do you like them apples! Talk about painting yourself a target!

Take, for example, the stand-offs between Jesus and the Pharisees over the issue of the Sabbath. Jesus specifically and defiantly broke the conventional religious laws relating to the observance of the Sabbath to demonstrate that religious systems were the means to an end, and not the end in and of itself. Luke 6 records two specific examples. With a seemingly well-intentioned value for a strict interpretation of the Mosaic covenant of Sabbath observance, the Pharisees set out to discredit Jesus by pointing to His lack of commitment to the law. In the first instance, Jesus and

His followers pick grain as they are walking through grain fields (v. 1). Luke specifically makes the point that the disciples are not farming, just innocently passing by grain as they were hungry and so they eat. Thinking they've caught Him red-handed in Sabbath breaking, the religious police accused them of harvesting on the day of rest, a clear disregard for one of the ten laws that God gave Moses for the people to remain in a right relationship with Him. Jesus, a blue-collar worker, responds to these religious scholars by saying, "*Haven't you read in the scriptures...?*" (Luke 6:3). The irony and mockery of Jesus' response is dripping, embarrassing sarcasm. A carpenter challenging the religious scholars with their knowledge of Scripture would be tantamount to a construction laborer publicly challenging the Attorney General with his knowledge of the law. Worse than pointing out their spiritual immaturity, Jesus ends His challenge by telling the Bible scholars of the day that He is "*Lord even over the Sabbath*" anyway (Luke 6:5)! He plays the ultimate trump card in this game by essentially informing the religious leaders that He was above their religious law.

Luke goes on to tell another story of Jesus disregarding the religious system in favor of fulfilling his job description and showing compassion. This time, He does it right in the synagogue – the physical representation of all things religious – and in plain view of the Pharisees who were watching Him closely. As He is teaching, Jesus conducts this little object lesson for the congregation. In the narrative, Luke describes how Jesus, knowing the thoughts of the Pharisees, pulls up a man who had a physical deformity (vs. 6-8). The man stands in front of everyone, and Jesus addresses the religious leaders in a public challenge of their religious value system. In front of everyone, He squares off against religious rulers and asks them a question this time. *"Does the law permit good deeds on the Sabbath, or is it a day for doing evil? Is this a day to save life or to destroy it?"* (Luke 6:9). Interpretation: "What is the point of your religious framework? Does the system exist for people or do the people exist for the system?" Answering His own question, Jesus tells the man to hold out his hand and, as he obeys, he is instantly healed. No wonder the very next verse says, *"At this, the enemies of Jesus* [the religious leaders] *were wild with rage and began to discuss what to do with him."* (Luke 6:11). They are more concerned with how they look in front of the people, their public image, than with the fact that the life of this deformed man is forever changed; such is the common symptom of religious propagation. Those with a priority for religious observance fall in the trap of being addicted to what people think of them. They are more concerned about maintaining a religious façade than with getting dirty while going about the real business of the Kingdom. Notice that with both of these examples of Jesus' pulling back the religious curtain He is doing so by practically caring for those who are hungry and oppressed. Consistent with the message of the prophets, Jesus exemplifies the truth that the spirituality God designed is a relationship with Him that evidences itself in social transformation. Jesus specifically bursts the religious bubble by showing that He came not for the religious but for the hungry and the poor.

Jesus represents the most scandalous, self-assured, irreligious, insubordinate, but hope filled symbol of real religion since the ancient time of the prophets. His most hostile, angry, and combative words are for the religious, not the irreligious. And as someone who has grown up in church, attended Bible school, and made his living by "professional" religious leadership, I am soberly and constantly aware of the fact that I represent a group that Jesus constantly antagonized. It is my colleagues whom Jesus referred to as "blind guides" (Matthew 15 & 23) and "sons of hell" (Matthew 23). Read the entirety of when Jesus hauled the pastors of the day over the coals:

> Then Jesus said to the crowds and to his disciples, "The teachers of religious law and the Pharisees are the official interpreters of the law of Moses. So practice and obey whatever they tell you, but don't follow their example. For they don't practice what they teach. They crush people with unbearable religious demands and never lift a finger to ease the burden. Everything they do is for show. On their arms they wear extra wide prayer boxes with Scripture verses inside, and they wear robes with extra long tassels. And they love to sit at the head table at banquets and in

the seats of honor in the synagogues. They love to receive respectful greetings as they walk in the marketplaces, and to be called 'Rabbi.' Don't let anyone call you 'Rabbi,' for you have only one teacher, and all of you are equal as brothers and sisters. And don't address anyone here on earth as 'Father,' for only God in heaven is your spiritual Father. And don't let anyone call you 'Teacher,' for you have only one teacher, the Messiah. The greatest among you must be a servant. But those who exalt themselves will be humbled, and those who humble themselves will be exalted. What sorrow awaits you teachers of religious law and you Pharisees. Hypocrites! For you shut the door of the Kingdom of Heaven in people's faces. You won't go in yourselves, and you don't let others enter either. What sorrow awaits you teachers of religious law and you Pharisees. Hypocrites! For you cross land and sea to make one convert, and then you turn that person into twice the child of hell you yourselves are! Blind guides... What sorrow awaits you teachers of religious law and you Pharisees. Hypocrites! For you are careful to tithe even the tiniest income from your herb gardens, but you ignore the more important aspects of the law—justice, mercy, and faith. You should tithe, yes, but do not neglect the more important things. Blind guides! You strain your water so you won't accidentally swallow a gnat, but you swallow a camel! What sorrow awaits you teachers of religious law and you Pharisees. Hypocrites! For you are so careful to clean the outside of the cup and the dish, but inside you are filthy—full of greed and self-indulgence! You blind Pharisee! First wash the inside of the cup and the dish, and then the outside will become clean, too. What sorrow awaits you teachers of religious law and you Pharisees. Hypocrites! For you are like whitewashed tombs—beautiful on the outside but filled on the inside with dead people's bones and all sorts of impurity. Outwardly you look like righteous people, but inwardly your hearts are filled with hypocrisy and lawlessness. What sorrow awaits you teachers of religious law and you Pharisees. Hypocrites! For you build tombs for the prophets your ancestors killed, and you decorate the monuments of the godly people your ancestors destroyed. Then you say, 'If we had lived in the days of our ancestors, we would never have joined them in killing the prophets.' But in saying that, you testify against yourselves that you are indeed the descendants of those who murdered the prophets. Go ahead and finish what your ancestors started. Snakes! Sons of vipers! How will you escape the judgment of hell? (Matthew 23:1-33)

So much for the flannel-graph, meek and mild, "Sunday School" Jesus. It is much safer not to be holding clergy credentials when Jesus is around. His posture with the "religious" and His posture with the "sinners" is accurately portrayed in the image of Him as a Lion and a Lamb. However, the conventional Western perception of Christians is much more reversed and in line with the priorities of the Pharisees. Today, Christians are more commonly thought to prefer the pious in-crowd and to cast judgment on the "sinners" of our day: the addicts, thieves, criminals, homeless, mentally ill, and even just socially awkward. Yet, it was the religious leaders Jesus condemned and who received His harshest judgments, and it was the sinners who were the objects of His patience and compassion, and most often the recipients of His company. Again, why are we, who bear His name today, not reputed for the same empathy and sympathy?

In 2008, a documentary was released called "Religulous." In it, the comedian Bill Maher travels the world looking for and interviewing religious people and leaders, mostly "Christians," in an effort to encapsulate the modern stereotype of religious values and practice.[1] The result was what you would expect from a comedian who wanted to use media to present a popularist, one-sided, agenda-driven, secular view of religion. However, the fact remains that the picture that Bill Maher paints of Christians, and religious people in general, is both accurate *and* far from the message and life of Christ, and I also believe that it's a stereotype we have earned. In a subsequent CBS interview, Maher is asked by the interviewer, "In the movie, you wished that Christians, if they were really Christians, would be more Christ-like."

Maher responds: "Don't we all? That's something I don't think is controversial. The message of Jesus, which is very good, is about love and forgiveness."[2] Maher's response also represents society's most prevailing critique and legitimate expectation of those who say they follow Christ. I have never heard anyone disagree with the message or the life of Jesus. The problem is that "Christians" in Western countries are not known for patterning their lives after the true message and the life of Christ.

From the book of Matthew alone, the message and the activities of Jesus include the following:

- Love for those who hate us (5:43-48).

- Giving to those in need (6:1-4).

- Not judging other people (7:1-6).

- Healing various people from leprosy, paralysis, blindness, high fever, and demonic influence (8:1-9:34).

- Feeding the hungry (15:32-38).

Why would anyone take exception to this type of person? Yet, why is it that today Christians are not recognized for having the same priorities? In his book *The Secret Message of Jesus*, Brian McLaren writes,

In healing the sick and raising the dead, in performing exorcisms and confronting injustice, in interacting miraculously with the forces of nature, Jesus even identifies himself with the story's original and ultimate hero – God – stating that those who had seen him had in some real way seen God, declaring that he and God were one, and suggesting that through him, God was launching a new world order, a new world, a new creation. These are not the words and ways of a polite teacher, no matter how brilliant. They go far beyond the claims of a typical priest, poet or philosopher – and even beyond the bold words of prophet or reformer. These are the primal, disruptive, inspiring, terrifying, shocking, hopeful words and ways of a revolutionary who seeks to overthrow the status quo in nearly every conceivable way.[3]

It is again time for the same message and the same revolution, one that isn't just the pipe dream of a utopian leader. It is a message and a revolution that clearly has its roots in God's original intent and was lived out in the words and life of God's Son while He was with us. The perfect man, Jesus, represents for us what is wonderfully possible in this life. The first man, Adam, represents humanity's fall into self-centered existence, including self-centered religion. However, the "second man," Jesus, reverses the effects of that fall and leads us into a redeemed existence that has nothing to do with institutional religion, but everything to do with a new relationship with God evidenced by a new social reality.

Christians who act like Christ, who truly and passionately do all they can to reflect the person of Jesus, shine out from the darkness of stale religion and present a refreshing compulsion for people to discover who it is they so obviously represent. Reading through the Gospels is undoubtedly the most condemning and most hope-filled exercise for those who are convinced that a massive transformation is necessary for Christ's-ones to be Christ-like.

It is hardly possible to talk about Jesus and the issue of compassion and justice without at least referring to His epic message about what the Kingdom of Heaven is like. In Matthew 22 and 25, Jesus teaches His closest followers about His Kingdom and He specifically contrasts it against the kingdom that is represented by the buildings on the temple grounds (Matthew 24:1). After using the temple buildings, the physical representation of all things religious, as an object lesson, Jesus sits down and explains to His inner circle what He means. Again, using the temple as the context, He starts His message by telling His disciples not to let anyone mislead them, and then goes on to discuss what will happen in the future. At the end of the message He leaves them with a crystal clear litmus test of who will be spending eternity with Him and who will be spending eternity with the Devil and his angels. This is not the stuff of systematic salvation theology. In fact, I used to struggle deeply with these words of Jesus, because they appear to be in contrast to other things He and Paul said and what I was taught about salvation theology. It's worth reading again:

When the Son of Man comes in his glory, and all the angels with him, then he will sit upon his glorious throne. All the nations will be gathered in his presence, and he will separate the people as a shepherd separates the sheep from the goats. He will place the sheep at his right hand and the goats at his left. Then the King will say to those on his right, 'Come, you who are blessed by my Father, inherit the Kingdom prepared for you from the creation of the world. For I was hungry, and you fed me. I was thirsty, and you gave me a drink. I was a stranger, and you invited me into your home. I was naked, and you gave me clothing. I was sick, and you cared for me. I was in prison, and you visited me.' Then these righteous ones will reply, 'Lord, when did we ever see you hungry and feed you? Or thirsty and give you something to drink? Or a stranger and show you hospitality? Or naked and give you clothing? When did we ever see you sick or in prison and visit you?' And the King will say, 'I tell you the truth, when you did it to one of the least of these my brothers and sisters, you were doing it to me!' Then the King will turn to those on the left and say, 'Away with you, you cursed ones, into the eternal fire prepared for the devil and his demons. For I was hungry, and you didn't feed me. I was thirsty, and you didn't give me a drink. I was a stranger, and you didn't invite me into your home. I was naked, and you didn't give me clothing. I was sick and in prison, and you didn't visit me.' Then they will reply, 'Lord, when did we ever see you hungry or thirsty or a stranger or naked or sick or in prison, and not help you?' And he will answer, 'I tell you the truth, when you refused to help the least of these my brothers and sisters, you were refusing to help me.' And they will go away into eternal punishment, but the righteous will go into eternal life. (Matthew 25:31-46)

My heart is moved and terrified every time I read Matthew 25. Without a good understanding of the whole Gospel and within the context of other teachings about salvation, this passage seems to be clear that entrance to Heaven is dependent on what we do for the poor. On first reading, it would appear that *if* we feed the hungry, clothe the naked, visit the sick and imprisoned, and house the homeless, we will go to Heaven. On the other hand, if we *don't* feed the hungry, clothe the naked, visit the sick and imprisoned, and house the homeless, we will go to Hell.

I don't believe for a moment that our good works gain us entrance to Heaven. Salvation, indeed, is God's unmerited work in our lives, not something we earn with our good works. However, what I do believe Jesus is clearly saying is that the *evidence* of whether or not someone is related to Him is in how they respond to the needs of the poor. Jesus does marry the reality of salvation in someone's life with the reality of selfless compassion. The preponderance of evidence as to whether or not we are redeemed is specifically and clearly demonstrated in how we treat specifically the hungry, thirsty, naked, sick, prisoner, and the homeless. More than that, Jesus tells us that if we don't practically love those in this socio-economic demographic, we don't love Him. I don't believe there is a more sobering message for the religious than this:

> He [Jesus] made it very clear that the proof of people's faith is not in the information they know or the religious gatherings they attend, but in the way they integrate what they know and believe into their every day practices. The hallmarks of the Church that Jesus died for are clear, based on Scripture: your profession of faith in Christ must be supported by a lifestyle that provides irrefutable evidence of your complete devotion to Jesus. The Lord encountered numerous people during His earthly tenure who could quote Scripture or pretend they knew and loved Him. But His reaction to them was always the same: "Show me the fruit."[4]

As the "second Adam" and perfect man, Jesus taught and lived the antithesis of the vacant religious shell that existed then and now. He echoed the message of the prophets and projected true religion on the main stage of daily living. He fulfilled His predestined job description as one that dispensed tangible grace-filled compassion in the margins of society, and reinforced that the Father has no time for religious structure without real substance. Jesus lived a life that constantly enabled and provided opportunities for people to reverse the effects of the Fall. The Kingdom that comprised the central messages and miracles of Jesus was demonstrated, not through alignment to the religious establishment, but instead by feeding the hungry, healing the sick, having intimacy with the marginalized, sending invitations to the outcast, extending generosity to the poor, and by the wealthy making radical sacrifices.

Moving from the Gospels into the life and rhythms of Jesus' earliest followers, the rest of the New Testament can be summed up by the very same call to today's Christians: be like Christ.

The Earliest Church – "All the believers were united in heart and mind. And they felt that what they owned was not their own, so they shared everything they had. The apostles testified powerfully to the resurrection of the Lord Jesus, and God's great blessing was upon them all. There were no needy people among them, because those who owned land or houses would sell them and bring the money to those in need" (Acts 4:32-35).

The most convincing evidence that a new reality is possible is found in what is written about the Church immediately after Christ ascended and the Holy Spirit fell upon His followers. Acts

2 and 4 give us two remarkably similar snapshots of what the early church was like and what the Church could be like again. If we want to get a picture of what a building is supposed to look like we need to refer to the blueprints, the original documents that provide for us a reference point for building. The Acts 2 and 4 portraits of the early church provide a reference point for those who want to know what the early church was about.

Here are some key phrases that tell us what this new community was like:

- a deep sense of awe

- signs and wonders

- united in heart and mind

- powerful

- shared everything they had

- sold what they owned

- great joy and generosity

- praising God and enjoying good will

- increase in their number

- God's great blessing was among them

- they gave

- there were no – did you get that – no needy people among them

Incredible! All the phrases that described the life of Christ also describe His first followers. This was visibly the community of Christ. This was the manifest presence of Jesus lived out through the community.

First, notice the spiritual reality that existed in the early church: there was a deep sense of awe and the display of signs and wonders. It was obvious that God's great blessing was among them. There was powerful witness to Christ's resurrection. They devoted themselves to prayer. They worshiped together each day. Their numbers increased each day. When was the last time you heard someone describing their church experience this way? When do we ever hear someone talk like this about their community of faith? We are happy if we can maintain status quo for attendance and giving from year to year. And we are thrilled if a handful of people every year decide to follow Christ or to be baptized. A good Sunday is one where a majority enjoys the sermon and the songs and the service doesn't get out too late. The criteria we regularly use to evaluate the health of the community of Christ are generally self-centered.

Second, notice the social atmosphere that existed in the early church. The word "shared" is used four times in five consecutive verses to describe the distribution of resources (Acts 2:42-46). They shared their meals. They even sold their homes and property and used the proceeds for those in need, creating an economic reality where there were no needy people among them. An even greater miracle, it says that *all* the believers were united in heart and mind. Again, when was the last time you heard people describe this as their social reality or church experience? The lamentable fact is that the norm in the Western local church is the *antithesis* of the picture found in Acts 2 and 4. Today, we even believe we are entitled to the exact opposite of the life described in the early church. We live in large homes with fences to keep out our neighbors. We have defined our wants as needs, just as those who don't follow Christ. We borrow money we don't have in order to buy what we don't need so that we don't have to share.

The 'me first' individual rights-oriented values have swallowed the Western Church, leaving it with little resemblance of what God intended. Over the past several decades, Western societies and governments have been so audacious as to equate our prosperity to God's approval. During the Cold War and immediately following, Western societies, which were ironically founded on biblical values, came to view as evil other societies which worked toward a communal balance. The Communist social motivation, while obviously subject to its own evils and corruption, isn't far from the ideal community described in Acts. The early roots of Communism were based upon a biblically similar motivation for equality and justice. However, growing up in North America, I came to interpret the economic success of our capitalist society as God being "on our side." God certainly has blessed developed countries, and the fundamental shortcomings of Communist ideology were firmly established by the political realities and history of Communism; nevertheless, I refuse to believe that God intended the Church to look the way it does in North America today or that somehow our political, economic, or social constructs are what God had in mind. Furthermore, the geo-political "us and them" mentality that ethnocentrically assumes God's support and approval is another stark contrast to the biblical picture of a compassionate Church.

Totally consistent with the Old Testament prophetic messages, the picture of the early church in Acts also leads to the conclusion that social transformation is an automatic by-product of spiritual transformation. Justice and compassion are the fruit on the tree of a vibrant spiritual experience, both individually and corporately. The Acts 2 and 4 pictures of the Church as a basket of spiritual fruit demonstrates that spiritual and social transformation can't be separated. If there is not fruit (justice and compassion) on the branches there is not life in the tree (Luke 13:6-8).

In 2002, I saw the powerful potential of what happens when followers of Christ today prioritize the generosity we read about in Acts. I was in a refugee camp in the middle of the Sahara Desert, working to get food and water to a group of people who had lived for more than a generation in the middle of the desert. They had been kicked out of their country more than 30 years prior and were forced to live in tents and mud homes in a neighboring country. There was only windswept sand as far as the eye could see. It was indeed the stereotypical "middle of nowhere." This displaced group of more than 150,000 Muslims,[5] is 100% dependant on foreign aid for survival. They are unable to grow any food and have very little access to water.

One evening we were sitting and speaking with a 30-year-old man who was our host. He was sharing about his life in the camps and his dreams for the future. He explained that one day he wanted to be a Christian. This was a significant statement to hear from a Muslim. We asked him why, as a Muslim man, did he want to follow Christ? He explained that for the 30 years of his life, living in these refugee camps, it had been people from "Christian" Western countries that have come and continued to send aid. He said, "We pray five times a day to Allah and nothing changes. Our Muslim brothers have forgotten about us out in the desert and it's the Christians that continue to help." It was an encouraging example of what is biblically and realistically possible again.

That evening our host prayed a simple prayer committing himself to following Christ. I have no idea to this day how much he understood his commitment, but I know he understood that something drew him toward the compassion he saw in followers of Christ. He desired to follow the Christ he saw in the Christians as opposed to what he didn't see in Islam. This powerful experience in the desert made these words of Jesus come to life in a way that must be replicated all over the globe:

> You're here to be light, bringing out the God-colors in the world. God is not a secret to be kept. We're going public with this, as public as a city on a hill. If I make you light-bearers, you don't think I'm going to hide you under a bucket, do you? I'm putting you on a light stand. Now that I've put you there on a hilltop, on a light stand—shine! Keep open house; be generous with your lives. By opening up to others, you'll prompt people to open up with God, this generous Father in heaven. (Matthew 5:15-17, The Message)

James – "Pure and genuine religion in the sight of God the Father means caring for orphans and widows in their distress and refusing to let the world corrupt you... What good is it, dear brothers and sisters, if you say you have faith but don't show it by your actions? Can that kind of faith save anyone? Suppose you see a brother or sister who has no food or clothing, and you say, "Good-bye and have a good day; stay warm and eat well"—but then you don't give that person any food or clothing. What good does that do? So you see, faith by itself isn't enough. Unless it produces good deeds, it is dead and useless" (James 1:27, 2:14-17).

James' book is written to believers everywhere, about practical faith lived out in day-to-day life. He is not writing to a specific context or responding to issues in any one church; he is not correcting particular problems evidenced in a certain community of faith.

In his passion to return to a theology and practice of salvation by faith alone, the reformer Martin Luther had a hard time with the book of James. Rejecting the theology and practice of merit-based salvation, he struggled whether or not to include it in the canon of Scripture. As with Matthew 25, it appears that James is saying that salvation is dependent on works. Yet, consistent with the message of Jesus, James is making an assumption that you cannot separate the evidence of faith from faith itself.

Consistent with the whole counsel of Scripture, James makes a point that should cause the North American Church to stop in its tracks and, in light of the global imbalance of resources, cause us to question our very salvation. In one of the few places that the word "religion" appears in the Bible, James' readers understood this word to mean the "outward demonstration of worship." In fact, the word used for "religion" in James 1:26 and 27 is a derivative of the word "worship".[6] Completely aligned with the Old Testament texts we considered, it could also be translated, "worship, as God sees it, is looking after those who are left alone without any way of providing for themselves."

In the context of providing for the poor, James says, "Faith without works is dead" (2:17). It doesn't get any clearer than that. Risking repetition, if the 20% of the world's population, who are from historically "Christian" nations, are consuming 80% of the world's resources, leaving the majority of the world's population to eke out an existence on 20% of the world's resources, Christian leaders from the West should be asking fundamental questions of self-examination. In view of James 2:17 and the gross imbalance of the world's resources, are we not, for the most part, representing and propagating a dead religious faith as opposed to the faith that presents itself as a transformed social reality? James identifies and condemns the same broken religious system as did the prophets and Jesus. Religion that can be content with the global status quo is frankly just that: religion.

Being despised and hated by society as a self-interested thief, after an encounter with Christ Zacchaeus, the tax collector, responds by giving half of his possessions to the poor (Luke 19:1-10). A relationship with Christ will result in the transformation of our attitudes about the poor and our possessions. Any claim that we follow Christ is stacked up against evidence of how we prioritize the needy and, in the absence of proof, observers have every reason to question the veracity of our faith. In his thorough work on what the Bible has to say about possessions and the poor, Craig Blomberg comments on the book of James:

The entire community is called to look out for the most dispossessed within its midst: the orphan, the widow or the person without adequate clothes or daily food. Those who even have a modest surplus of goods with which they could help the destitute, but who refused to do so, prove thereby that they are not truly Christian, regardless of any profession they may make.[7]

The Writings of Paul – "In fact, James, Peter, and John, who were known as pillars of the church, recognized the gift God had given me, and they accepted Barnabas and me as their co-workers. They encouraged us to keep preaching to the Gentiles, while they continued their work with the Jews. Their only suggestion was that we keep on helping the poor, which I have always been eager to do" (Galatians 2:9-11).

Genuine concern for the poor was also evident in Paul's ministry and travel. In Galatians, his earliest letter,[8] Paul affirms and promotes what has already become abundantly evident in the early church: a dynamic spirituality very much includes specific concern for the needy that results in action. Consistent with the rest of Scripture, Paul speaks often about possessions, healthy spirituality, and caring for the poor. In Romans 15, the community of God in Macedonia and Achaia *"eagerly took up an offering for the poor among the believers in Jerusalem"* (v. 26). In Galatians 2, the disciples of Jesus encouraged Paul, in his ministry of preaching, to *"keep on helping the poor"* (v. 11), which Paul affirms as a priority for his itinerant ministry.

In addition to the direct mention of the poor within Paul's ministry, his teaching and preaching advocates a spirituality lived out in direct opposition to the social and religious system of the day. In Romans, he explains that Jesus breaks the back of sin and self, freeing us to live out the love we have been shown (Romans 6-8). In 1 Corinthians 13, Paul warns the Church against spiritual pride and divisions, and explains that a life of love is the evidence of true spirituality. In 2 Corinthians 8, the apostle calls the Church to a life of generosity toward those who are suffering. In Ephesians, he lays out how a spirit-filled life will impact relationships we have with our families, churches, and workplaces. In Philippians, he powerfully describes what it means to live as "citizens of Heaven" in contrast to living as citizens of this world:

> Is there any encouragement from belonging to Christ? Any comfort from his love? Any fellowship together in the Spirit? Are your hearts tender and compassionate? Then make me truly happy by agreeing wholeheartedly with each other, loving one another, and working together with one mind and purpose. Don't be selfish; don't try to impress others. Be humble, thinking of others as better than yourselves. Don't look out only for your own interests, but take an interest in others, too. You must

have the same attitude that Christ Jesus had. Though
he was God, he did not think of equality with God as
something to cling to. Instead, he gave up his divine
privileges; he took the humble position of a slave and was
born as a human being. When he appeared in human
form, he humbled himself in obedience to God and died
a criminal's death on a cross. (Philippians 2:1-8)

Here, Paul asks if belonging to Christ makes any difference
in the life of believers. Then he answers his own question: the
life of those who belong to Christ is evidenced by self-emptying
love versus self-centered living. If there was anything ambiguous
in the Old Testament writings about the role of compassion in
spirituality, the New Testament focuses even more solidly on
the issue. The words of Jesus, Luke, Paul, and James leave no
room for a spirituality that does not result in an individual and
corporate life of compassion and justice.

Now, viewing the global imbalance of resources and the
unjust economic realities we discussed in Part One through the
lens of a biblical picture of a compassionate community of God
in Part Two, we have discovered a serious problem: the Church in
North America today is clearly living far from the biblical vision
of compassion and justice. Our existence at the beginning of this
third millennium appears soberingly similar to the lifeless forms
of empty religion found at various times in the Old and New
Testaments.

Writing about the big picture of the brokenness of the world and of the Western Church, I recognize I run the risk of being interpreted as saying churches are doing nothing of any value. But these are not black-and-white issues. We can all think of churches that raise money for missionaries, missions projects, and "needs at home." In His exceptional graciousness, God uses the gatherings of His people to impact lives for His Kingdom. Obviously, not all Western churches or Christians are hedonistic or narcissistic. However, the realities we find in the world and in the Church today, as well as what we read in so much of Scripture, lead to the conclusion that there is potential for so much more.

Other than a few exceptionally bright spots of churches and leaders who have caught the vision and opportunity for change, the priorities of the Western Church as a whole mirror that of Western culture. We take our "me-first" materialistic consumer way of life into the Kingdom of God. We are not different from our culture as was the call of the prophets. Our priorities are to have "church" in a way that aligns with our preferences and the vast majority of time and money is spent working toward that end. Compassion and social justice, locally or globally, are relegated to the leftover crumbs of our time and resources. The respectable norm is to take a "benevolent fund" offering once a month to keep some dry food stocked in the church pantry. We leave social action to the social activists, who are usually considered fringe to the mainstream church or even liberal. We leave global poverty for the politicians and large non-governmental organizations to figure out and address. We are usually moved only by the catastrophic emergencies, like the Indian Ocean Tsunami of Boxing Day 2004 or Hurricane Katrina in 2005, that capture our attention for as long as the cameras are rolling, responding with token, one-time giving until the next time. This type of "response" is no different from that of those who claim no allegiance to Christ.

Clearly, the status quo is spiritually perilous. We are in desperate need of radical transformation!

Chapter 6 - So now what?

1. Which New Testament passage(s) impacted you the most?

2. Do you see a consistent thread or principle being taught in these passages of Scripture? What is it?

3. Why do you think that institutional religion loses a priority to care for the poor?

4. What similarities do you see between the institution of the Pharisees and the institution of the Church today?

5. If you wandered around with Jesus today, where do you think you would go and what kinds of things would you do?

6. Why were people attracted to Jesus and repelled by His contemporary religious leaders?

7. If most Christians today made a determined effort to really look and act like Christ, what effect do you think it would have in our community and country?

8. What are some practical ways your church could look more like the Church in Acts 2 and 4?

9. Why do you think a personal encounter with Jesus specifically impacts how we treat the poor?

PART THREE – THE CORE CHANGES
NECESSARY FOR TRANSFORMATION

Chapter 7

Change

Change vs. Behavior Modification

Nothing short of a historical, comprehensive, and prevailing transformation is required to wake the Western Church from her catatonic state in a way that would tip the scales of global resources. Only a massive renovation of the heart could facilitate the provision of the most basic needs of half of the world's population, a transformation that is characterized by an undeniable revival of whole spirituality and a breathtaking reality of global compassion and social justice.

It is not an option to simply tweak what we are currently doing, or make programmatic adjustments to the status quo and hope things will change. I am not talking about making church more attractive to outsiders and giving a little more money to charity. As the saying goes, "Insanity is continuing to do the same thing while expecting different results." The road we are on today as a North American Church mirrors the same religious road traveled by God's people in the Old and New Testaments and the same total repentance is necessary.

The genesis of a renovated world is a revived Church. The level of spiritual degradation that describes the Western Church will not be turned around by guilt-driven media or more pictures of starving kids on TV. Change that has its roots in behavior modification rarely lasts. Greater awareness of the need will not bring about this kind of transformation. We all know there are starving people in the world and there is something in all of us that knows it's wrong. Efforts to address poverty and injustice usually start with talk of behavioral change, but they rarely end in the type of action that makes a difference.

At the same time, there is a growing awareness that the current manifestation of church doesn't represent Christ. There is a wave of pew-warmers convinced that there has to be more to church and life than our current experiences; and there exists a nagging, underlying feeling that the gospel we read about must address the most pressing needs and suffering in our world. This pressure cooker that combines spiritual discontent and a growing indignation toward the imbalance we've allowed to persist represents the most hopeful opportunity for change. In his book *Revolution*, George Barna accurately describes this emerging reason for hope. Writing about those who are fed up with the current state of the Church, he says:

> They have no use for churches that play religious games, whether those games are worship services that drone on without the presence of God or ministry programs that bear no spiritual fruit. Revolutionaries eschew ministries that compromise or soft sell our sinful nature to expand organizational turf. They refuse to follow people in ministry leadership positions who cast a personal vision rather than God's, who seek popularity rather than the proclamation of truth in their public statements, or who are more concerned about their own legacy than that of Jesus Christ. They refuse to donate one more dollar to man-made monuments that mark their own achievements and guarantee their place in history. They are unimpressed by accredited degrees and endowed chairs in Christian colleges and seminaries that produce young people incapable of defending the Bible or unwilling to devote their lives to serving others. And Revolutionaries are embarrassed by language that promises Christian love and holiness but turns out to be all sizzle and no substance. The experience provided through their churches seems flat. They are seeking a faith experience that is more robust and awe inspiring, a spiritual journey that prioritizes transformation at every turn, something

worthy of the Creator whom their faith reflects. They are seeking the spark provided by a commitment to a true revolution in thinking, behavior and experience where settling for what is merely good and above average is defeat.[1]

What is happening is not just an acknowledgement that we must act differently or that our programs need to change. Our hearts are changing. Our default Western core values must be and are being transformed. Our spiritual DNA is being altered to reflect counter-cultural biblical values. As agents of change, our focus must be on deep, spiritual metamorphosis and not just on behavioral symptoms. And, as we have already identified, spiritual transformation evidences itself in social transformation. The situation is too dire and so far beyond our ability to change that we have no other choice but to submit to a spiritual heart transplant, not just a bypass or temporary fix.

Core Values

As leaders, we must stop trying to talk people out of sinning or self-centered lifestyle choices. Trying to sell the benefits of sacrifice or commitment will only last as long as the next choice to prioritize self over God or others. Instead, we must focus on fostering a desire for something greater than self. We have to fan each little flame into a roaring, passionate fire for intimacy with God and His Kingdom. When we foster that greater desire, we will see people's choices and behaviors fall in line with the greater desire of their hearts for the glory of God and His fame among the nations.

As a leader and former pastor, I am tired of trying to convince people to be more committed or convince them that they shouldn't sin. I believe that spiritual leaders in the West are burning themselves out trying to figure out new ways to get people to sign up for marginally successful programs and increase their giving to meet the church budget. All of us act on what we believe the most: our personal and corporate core values determine our action or inaction. If we want to see real and pervasive transformation both inside the Western Church and in a world desperate for that Church's mission, we, as followers of Christ, must focus on transforming the core values in our lives. Many leaders are currently writing and speaking about the need for change, further convincing us all that what we have is broken and ineffective. However, I don't believe merely telling everyone about the need to change serves the Church or the world in a significant way. Change happens when people *desire* a new reality more than the current reality. When people see a potential future more preferable than the present, a sense of urgency grows in anticipation of the first steps toward change.

How do we actually move beyond a conviction that everything must change and toward a rediscovery of a dynamic spiritual experience that manifests again the Acts 2 and 4 vision?

We urgently need to discover how to ensure the history book written about the North American Church in the twenty-first century reads as follows: "The Western Church was radically transformed from a lethargic, overfed, ineffective institution to a force of love and compassion that changed the world. Local churches became gatherings of awe and wonder, signs and miracles. Churches of various traditions and forms of worship were unified around a common vision and mission. Followers of Christ moved away from a culture of consumerism to sacrificial giving, even selling their personal and corporate possessions so that their global neighbors could have access to the basics of life. Needless suffering was essentially eradicated because of a redistribution of resources and concentrated, coordinated efforts of immediate relief and sustainable community development. Once again the Church became a respected voice of credibility in the world, realized by its reputation for love and compassion. It transformed the world by rediscovering and manifesting Christ-like priorities and action."

I am confident that God has already given us all we need for this kind of history to be written about the Church and the world in this next generation. However, each of us must make a very personal commitment to allow our hearts to be transformed in a way that affects our hands and feet. Meditate on the mind-blowing potential of what Paul says to the church in Ephesus:

I pray that your hearts will be flooded with light so that you can understand the confident hope he has given to those he called – his holy people who are his rich and glorious inheritance. I also pray that you will understand the incredible greatness of God's power for us who believe in him. This is the same mighty power that raised Christ from the dead and seated him in the place of honor at God's right hand in the heavenly realms. (Ephesians 1:18-20)

Don't read that so quickly. Do you realize that the same power that raised Christ from the dead is available for us? Can you imagine the potential of the community of God who realizes this and lives it out? Our spiritual vacancy is an opportunity. Our hunger and thirst for spiritual substance over religious form makes us candidates for God's activity in our lives. The more desperate we become for God, the closer we move toward the river of spiritual life. Keeping in mind the growing chorus of discontent among His followers at the state of the institutional Church and the world, listen to the hope-filled words of Jesus: *"God blesses those who are poor and realize their need for him, for the Kingdom of Heaven is theirs...God blesses those who hunger and thirst for justice, for they will be satisfied. God blesses those who are merciful, for they will be shown mercy...God blesses those who work for peace, for they will be called children of God"* (Matthew 5:3, 6-7, 9). We must move beyond the desire for change and start living out the change, understanding that it will cost us our excessive comfort, safety, and security. There can be no revolution without cost. We must have bold, visionary, risk-taking, and self-emptying leadership that exemplifies a non-conformist transformation.

At the same time, I want to be careful not to foster an expectation that if we simply apply a religious formula we will get a predetermined result. We can't make God work. We can't make Him change anything or act within our timelines. However, God's sovereignty is not an excuse for our inactivity. The reality is that there are clear "if/then" sections of Scripture that tell us if we do such-and-such then God will do what He does, in His perfect time. God's activity in our lives and in this world is carried out in concert with our obedience as His children. God makes His power and presence conditional on us holding up our end of the bargain.

The very culture of the Western Church must change if we ever hope to make an impact on this world commensurate with our resources and realistic potential. A culture is simply a shared set of values and resulting behavior. We need a rediscovery of the shared set of values that the Holy Spirit works into the process of our becoming like Christ. And we require an understanding of the transformational potential that exists in those who follow Him. In the next chapters, we will look at the core values that must change if we are to realize the vision of a Church that could transform the world.

Chapter 7 - So now what?

1. Why do most of our efforts at personal change often seem so short-lived?

2. Why is corporate change (churches, denominations, businesses, etc.) often so difficult?

3. Why do you think compassion and social justice is becoming important to our society, both inside and outside the Church?

4. Think of a person (you or someone else) that has tried many times to change something in their life. Why has the change been so difficult?

5. Why do you think people resist change, even when they would agree that the outcome of the change is more preferable than their current reality?

6. Think of a person or a group of people that have made a major change in their lives. Why were they successful in changing?

7. What must happen for you or for your church to become more tangibly compassionate or outwardly focused?

8. What will a life of compassion and justice cost in a specific situation that needs your involvement?

Chapter 8

The Holy Spirit, Prayer, and Worship

The Invading Holy Spirit

In our own power, we are simply incapable of producing the kind of change we long for. Although we are alive in Christ, the effects of sin cause us to be hardwired with a propensity for self. We often read about the church at the end of Acts 2 without really knowing how it was they were able to persevere the way they did. In a relatively short time, one chapter to be exact, the followers of Christ went from an obscure group of spiritual misfits to a force of wonder, power, love, and compassion that was drawing incredible numbers. It was the Pharisees' worst nightmare. They were really hoping that they had put down this religious insurrection with the crucifixion of Christ and that religious life would return to the religious status quo. Instead, this movement seemed to be even more powerful and popular than before. It was a community characterized by awe, and accompanied by signs and wonders. Those who were struggling to make ends meet were cared for in a practical way that brought about socioeconomic equalization and personal value. And, not surprisingly, each day people were being attracted to this new movement. But how? What brought about the dramatic change from a fringe group of scared, untrained, and unqualified young men and women to the rediscovered organic movement that God intended?

We can't begin to understand Acts 2:42-47 (a different social reality), without Acts 2:1-4 (a different spiritual reality). We can't experience the end of Acts 2 without experiencing the beginning of Acts 2:

> All the believers were meeting together in one place. Suddenly, there was a sound from heaven like the roaring of a mighty windstorm, and it filled the house where they were sitting. Then, what looked like flames or tongues of fire appeared and settled on each of them. And everyone present was filled with the Holy Spirit. (Acts 2:1-4)

The power for their transformation came from the Holy Spirit. Being occupied by the Holy Spirit was a means to a transformed and powerful end. In themselves, they were weak, defeated, ineffective, and marginalized. But when the Outside Force invaded their individual lives, they became a powerful army of compassion and justice, reflecting the life and priorities of their Founder and Friend. Peter, for example, started out being "all talk and no substance" before the filling of the Spirit; then he heals a man who was a beggar crippled from birth (Acts 3:1-11); he later preaches right in the temple, the religious center stage that got Jesus in hot water with the leaders, telling them that the Jesus they crucified was raised from the dead (Acts 3:12-26); and he is eventually hauled in front of the religious police where he boldly declares that he is much more concerned about obeying God rather than men (Acts 4:1-22). The change was dramatic in Peter. No one could deny that *something* had happened to cause such a transformation.

Instead of calling upon and waiting to be filled with the Holy Spirit, we are much more inclined to look for new earthly techniques and methods to improve our effectiveness today. Rather than declaring our dependence, we look around us to see what others are doing, thinking that if we mirror successful programs or copy other leaders, we too, will grow our church or our ministries. And, while learning from others is helpful, and seeking conventional wisdom is biblically justifiable, we have become dependent on the commercialization of religious methods rather than on the power of the Holy Spirit to affect change in society and the world.

To use an inadequate illustration, it would be like investing time and money building a stunning car and forgetting about the engine that moves it forward. We become content to push it around ourselves, or we tie it to the movement of another car for our momentum. We are all impressed that it looks so good, without being concerned about its ability to actually go anywhere. We are caught up with form while forgetting about substance. Another way of illustrating the state of the Western Church is as an impressive banquet without providing significant nourishment. We secure a great banquet room, decorate beautifully, pull out the finest silverware, china, and crystal, but we forget about feeding the people when they come, spiritually or physically. And then when people stop coming, we think we need to improve on the trappings to bring them back or to prevent them from going to someone else's house for dinner.

We have grown accustomed to and dependent on our human effort and man-made forms. Just as the nation of Israel in the Old Testament and the Pharisees of the New Testament, what we have left is an institutional religion that spends the majority of its resources perpetuating ceremony. As we examined in Part One, the spiritual bankruptcy of the Western Church and the physical bankruptcy of the developing world has regressed too far to be rescued by greater human effort, education, discussions, consultations, seminars, and conferences alone. Spiritual transformation must precede social transformation. Our passion for Christ and His priorities will lead us into a life of compassion.

Throughout history, social change has followed great spiritual revivals or awakenings. Social change was a spillover effect of revival. Listen to the results of the Welsh revival of 1904:

> Countless numbers of souls were saved. No records were kept of the actual number converted, but 150,000 is a very conservative estimate during the first six months. Not only were individual lives changed by the power of the Holy Spirit, but whole communities were changed, indeed society itself was changed. Public houses (pubs) became almost empty. Men and women who used to waste their money in getting drunk were now saving it, giving it to help their churches, buying clothes and food for their families. And not only drunkenness, but stealing and other offences grew less and less so that often a magistrate came to court and found there were no cases for him. Men whose language had been filthy before learnt to talk purely. The ponies were so used to being cursed and sworn at that they just didn't understand when orders were given in kind, clean words! The dark tunnels underground in the mines echoed with the sounds of prayer and hymns, instead of oaths and nasty jokes and gossip. People who had been careless about paying their bills, or paying back money they had borrowed, paid up all they owed. People who had not been friends for a long

time because of something that had happened in the past, forgot their quarrels and were happy together again.[1]

Monastic orders and spiritual movements were often characterized by simplicity, devotion, and service to the poor. A classic example is that of St. Francis of Assisi who is known for having said, "Preach the gospel at all times – if necessary use words." He left a worldly life and the military around 1205 to live a life of simplicity, even poverty, in order to live among the poor to "bear witness to a Christian life".[2] In 1521, Ignatius of Loyola, a young, upper-class soldier from Spain, echoed the life and mission of St. Francis by forming the Society of Jesus to live among and serve the poor.[3]

Near the end of the Great Awakening in 1743, Jonathan Edwards recounted the revival and the resulting social effects:

> Ever since the great work of God that was wrought here about nine years ago, there has been a great abiding alteration in this town in many respects. There has been vastly more religion kept up in the town, among all sorts of persons, in religious exercises and in common conversation than used to be before. There has remained a more general seriousness and decency in attending the public worship. There has been a very great alteration among the youth of the town with respect to reveling, frolicking, profane and unclean conversation, and lewd

songs. Instances of fornication have been very rare. There has also been a great alteration among both old and young with respect to tavern haunting. I suppose the town has been in no measure so free of vice in these respects for any long time together for this sixty years as it has been this nine years past. There has also been an evident alteration with respect to a charitable spirit to the poor (though I think with regard to this in this town, as the land in general, come far short of Gospel rules). And though after that great work nine years ago there has been a very lamentable decay of religious affections and the engagedness of people's spirit in religion, yet many societies for prayer and social religion were all along kept up; and there were some few instances of awakening and deep concern about the doings of another world, even in the most dead time.[4]

These are only a few examples of what happens when spiritual revival, a new work of the Holy Spirit, takes place in situations characterized by spiritual and social depravity. People, predominantly young leaders, become undone by what *is* compared to what *should* be, and can't help but call on God to act. The pain of the sacrifice becomes less than the pain of letting things continue as they are. Emerging leaders have a greater desire for change, and all it means, than for the things of this world. The spiritual void becomes a place for the Holy Spirit to fill.

Consequently, the society can't help but be changed by a Church that is consumed by the Spirit's power and Christ's priorities.

In all of our cause-related angst about the global imbalance of resources, poverty, and injustice, we can't begin to hope for a response that is equal to the need without first recognizing that our spiritual poverty has vastly contributed to creating such imbalance. The materialistic hedonism that has gripped the Western Church, right along with the rest of Western society, is both a symptom of our spiritual impoverishment and a cause of the extreme suffering that grips half the world's population. While it is an encouraging development that there are many people these days writing and talking about the world's great needs and the Church's woefully inadequate response, we still fall short of digging deep enough for real transformation to occur. The world will not be affected by simply sponsoring more children or by sending people to more websites that advocate for the poor, although these are baby steps in the right direction. We have to first recognize the spiritual problem with the Church before we can ever hope to address the social problems of the nations.

I seriously question the continued effectiveness of the traditional missionary model that has been the norm for the past 100 years. This approach is based on the assumption that we in the Western Church have our spiritual "ducks in a row" before we can help others know Christ. This was never clearer to me than when I first got off an airplane in sub-Saharan Africa. As

I referred earlier, my task on this trip was to assist a local rural African pastor to get a small primary health care clinic up and running with support from a Canadian funding partner. On the two-hour drive along red dirt roads from the small airport to the rural village, I asked the pastor about the history of his work among the people. In our discussion about his work and the need for a proper health care facility, he told me about a lady in his church whose sister was lying sick in a hovel of a clinic. There was no proper diagnostic equipment or means with which to treat this woman. After some time, word came to the pastor that the sister had died, so he decided to go to the clinic to comfort his grieving parishioner.

He walks into the clinic and pulls back a curtain that surrounds an exam table, finding the dead woman lying there and the grieving sister sitting on the floor. After consoling the woman, my new pastor friend decides to leave the clinic and go back to the church to make the preparations for a funeral. As he walks out of the clinic, he hears the voice of God telling him to go back inside and pray for the dead woman. He begins to argue with God, reminding Him that the woman is already dead and that praying for her would only further grieve the sister and be a bad witness to the health care workers who would see this. But again, the voice of God tells him to go back and pray for the dead woman. So, he reluctantly obeys and heads back in. As he lays hands on the dead woman, he notices her body has become cold and stiff. Then he prays, "God, you are the same yesterday, today, and forever. Sister, in the name of Jesus, arise." As he prays that prayer, the woman's eyes immediately open but she isn't breathing. So he continues to pray, "Sister, I said, in the name of Jesus, arise." And as he finishes this prayer, her lungs fill with air and he helps her to sit up. He turns to the medical workers and says, "Here is your patient."

I sat in silence, listening to him tell me this story in a way that made me think this type of ministry was not abnormal there. I had only been on African soil for about an hour before I'm hearing about a woman being raised from the dead. God's amazing power worked through this diminutive rural pastor to perform signs and wonders we unfortunately only read about in Scripture. I asked myself, "What in the world do I have to offer this man? It should be him getting off an airplane in my country, me picking him up and taking him to tell these stories to churches in the West." It was another defining realization of how spiritually vacant and numb the body of Christ is where I come from, so jarring that my jealousy of this servant of God added to an already acute discontent with my church experience.

If the Western Church ever hopes to become the force of power and justice we were meant to be, we first must acknowledge our absolute need for God's dramatic intervention and get on our knees to call for the Spirit to visit us again. We must pray as Isaiah prayed:

Oh, that you would burst from the heavens and come down! How the mountains would quake in your presence! As fire causes wood to burn and water to boil, your coming would make the nations tremble...When you came down long ago, you did awesome deeds beyond our highest expectations. (Isaiah 64:1-3)

Prayer and Worship

While a dramatic visitation of the Holy Spirit upon the Western Church would immediately create the kind of spiritual and social transformation we envision, we cannot simply sit around, passively waiting for a revival to affect change. The death and resurrection of Christ opened the curtain for us to have direct access to the presence of God, and He loves our communion with Him more than we can imagine. It is in the intimacy of His presence where our lives are changed, formed into the image of Christ. And it is the image of Christ that the world so desperately needs to see in the darkness of incredible preventable suffering:

> But whenever someone turns to the Lord, the veil is taken away. For the Lord is the Spirit, and wherever the Spirit of the Lord is, there is freedom. So all of us who have had that veil removed can **see and reflect the glory of the Lord. And the Lord—who is the Spirit—makes us more and more like him as we are changed into his glorious image.** (2 Corinthians 3:16-18, emphasis added)

The passage you just read is the summary of this book. Seeing and reflecting. The signs are everywhere that the Church in the West doesn't look like Christ. Any hope of becoming like Him is in seeing and then reflecting His image. We must seek God for a great awakening, and become consumed by the daily pursuit of His presence. God is salting the tongues of a generation, making us crave the river of His presence as a means of both reviving His people and bringing about His Kingdom on this earth. Looking at the landscape of North American Christianity, George Barna makes the following comment regarding what is stirring in the Church:

> The new revolution...the personal renewal and recommitment of believers. The dominant catalyst is people's desperation for a genuine relationship with God. The renewal of that relationship spurs believers to participate in the spreading of the gospel. Rather than relying on a relative handful of inspired preachers to promote a national revival, the emerging revolution is truly a grassroots explosion of commitment to God that will refine the Church and result in a natural and widespread immersion in outreach...In the end, the revolution transforms believers so that they can transform the world...The very life of the believer becomes a means of worship and outreach.[5]

This personal renewal is wrought in the simplicity of seeking the face of God through both personal and corporate prayer and worship. When I am in the presence of God, He exchanges my self-centered values for Christ-like priorities. Sadly, though, prayer has become another religious duty: "I should" instead of "I must." And worship has grossly become synonymous with the music on a Sunday morning before the message. Our hedonistic value system prevents prayer from ever becoming a priority. We'd never say this out loud, but our decision making goes something like this: "If it doesn't immediately benefit me in some way, I'd rather not, thanks." We don't pray because we don't feel like praying. And the temptation of leaders (and I'm including myself) is to find new and creative ways to entice people into the spiritual discipline of prayer, to convince them to want to pray. We feel the pressure to make prayer more attractive or more… fun. And, if that doesn't work, we can always fall back to the "we should" guilt motivation. As in marriage, for example, when the relationship is strong and intimate we don't need to muster the motivation to communicate. However, when a relationship has been neglected, communication and interaction are relegated to an item on a list of tasks. Unless we completely recognize our need for God to intervene in our lives and in the broken situations of our world, we will continue to wallow in the soul-deadening mediocrity of religious observance.

In contrast to our current version, let's consider the biblical reality of worship and prayer as an undeniable conduit of Kingdom activity:

- While **Abram was in prayer**, God told him to leave and go to a place that God would later show him (Genesis 12).

- **God met with Moses** at the bush to discuss with him the plan for delivering the Israelites out of Egypt (Exodus 3).

- While **Moses had his hands lifted**, God's army was winning the battle (Exodus 17).

- **Moses met with God** to figure out what to do when the people were worshiping the golden calf (Exodus 32).

- While the Israelites ran into the walls of Jericho, got scared, and wanted to go back to Egypt, **Joshua got alone with God** to find out what to do (Joshua 5).

- **Samson went to God** for the power to get revenge on the Philistines (Judges 16).

- When the Israelites wanted a king, **Samuel prayed to the Lord** to find out what He wanted (1 Samuel 8).

- As the enemy was advancing on Elisha, **he prayed** and then God struck the people with blindness (2 Kings 6).

- Before many notable manifestations of God's power, **Jesus Himself went off alone to pray** (Luke 6 & Matthew 26).

- When Peter and John were before the Sanhedrin, Acts says that when the leaders saw the courage of Peter and John, they realized that these were unschooled, ordinary men **and took note that these men had been with Jesus** (Acts 4).

Time and time again, nothing significant happened independent of prayer, yet today we act as if prayer is a polite consideration to God. If the state of the Western Church and the state of global injustice is as I have summarized in Part One, then our only hope to turn the tide is an extraordinarily unified and concerted effort to pray. Prayer is the hope-filled acknowledgement of our complete dependence on God for personal and corporate transformation. God consistently allows His people to muddle around in their efforts until they recognize their need for His transforming power. Prayer changes the heart of the one who prays and brings about the intervention of God in the affairs of humankind.

In the New Testament book of James about how faith is lived out in the common daily realities of life, the writer inextricably joins spiritual life with social life:

What is causing the quarrels and fights among you? Don't they come from the evil desires at war within you? You want what you don't have, so you scheme and kill to get it. You are jealous of what others have, but you can't get it, so you fight and wage war to take it away from them. Yet you don't have what you want because you don't ask God for it. And even when you ask, you don't get it because your motives are all wrong—you want only what will give you pleasure. You adulterers! Don't you realize that friendship with the world makes you an enemy of God? I say it again: If you want to be a friend of the world, you make yourself an enemy of God. What do you think the Scriptures mean when they say that the spirit God has placed within us is filled with envy? But he gives us even more grace to stand against such evil desires. As the Scriptures say, "God opposes the proud but favors the humble." So humble yourselves before God. Resist the devil, and he will flee from you. Come close to God, and God will come close to you. Wash your hands, you sinners; purify your hearts, for your loyalty is divided between God and the world. Let there be tears for what you have done. Let there be sorrow and deep grief. Let there be sadness instead of laughter, and gloom instead of joy. Humble yourselves before the Lord, and he will lift you up in honor. (James 4:1-10)

Apparently, there is an intimate relationship between drawing near to God and how we live with those around us. Independence from God aligns us with the world's priorities, but intimacy with God results in the power and motivation to renovate the status quo. God's closeness to His people, through the conduit of worship and prayer, alters the social reality we find ourselves in.

Far too many activists and social engineers focus on creating change by altering how people act without paying attention to why people are motivated to act the way they do. If our personal values mirror the values of the world, we will live out those values as the world does. But instead, if our personal values mirror those of Christ, if our priorities are aligned to His, our actions will be too. We don't pray only for God to intervene and change the social reality around us. We pray primarily so that God would change us to live out a new social reality around us. The pursuit of closeness, of an intimacy with God, will foster in us a greater desire for selfless compassion than for self-centered priorities and lifestyle choices. Again, I can't stress this point enough. Efforts at social change, justice, and compassion that are not rooted in spiritual transformation will be truncated and ineffective. The kind of renovation that is needed to produce lasting change will only come about by spiritual transformation. The immensity of the world's pain and unnecessary suffering in the face of the West's abundance of resources forces us to go to the only One who can change that reality. Our inability to effect the necessary change brings about the compulsion to call on the One who can.

About ten years ago, I was going through a time in my ministry where I looked around me and saw nothing but spiritual scarcity. I read about the New Testament Church and was deeply frustrated by the fact that my ministry was more like a religious daycare center than a powerful force of love and change in people's lives. It seemed like everyone who came to me for spiritual guidance was also frustrated by the lack of power for holy living and effective service. I was completely aggravated by the fact that Christ promised that we who believe in Him would do the same things that Christ did, and in fact would do greater things (John14:12). I was confused: why, if the same power that raised Christ from the dead lived in us (Ephesians 1:19-20), was there so little evidence of that power in the lives and ministries around me?

It was during that time that I first saw Jim Cymbala's sermon called, My *House Shall Be Called a House of Prayer*. The Gospels record the righteous anger of Jesus when He violently throws out the religious busybodies, reminding everyone of the purpose of the house of God: prayer. I was broken by the painful realization that God passionately desires to pour out His power in people's lives but my prayerlessness and reliance on manmade programs left Him out of the equation. There was no power because there was no prayer. Corporately, there is very little power in the Church because there is very little prayer in the Church.

In Matthew, Mark, and Luke we see a completely unique and, frankly, scary side of Jesus when He cleared the temple. Consistent with His antagonistic posture to organized religion, He blows up and violently makes His point about His Father's intent for the gathering of His people. Even though the buying and the selling in the temple was permitted for the specific purpose of providing animals for sacrifice, the religious leaders were again completely missing the point of God's instruction. While the religious activities were many, Jesus wanted them to realize that God's intent for the temple was that it be a house of prayer, for intimacy with Him. And again today, we have replaced God's original intent with many other activities. Our church buildings or places of ministry are houses of many activities other than prayer. We have made them into houses of preaching, teaching, music, programs, and banquets, but we have not made them into houses of prayer. Again, these are all good activities for us to engage in, as was the provision of animals for temple sacrifices, but we must not forget the objective of all of these activities. If we announce a potluck dinner or a good musical group, people will come. If we announce a prayer meeting, precious few will come. The aroma of prayer is to characterize and even define the gathered people of God. The prayers of God's people are the conduit of God's power and grace to infect and affect the lives of people. By far, the majority of time and emotional energy of the Western Church is spent on everything but prayer. We have come to depend on programs, education, strategies, degrees, books, and even relevance to affect change. We have nudged God out of His Kingdom's work by how educated, planned, programmed, and relevant we are. In stark contrast, God moved and displayed His power and presence in circumstances of weakness, of the average, marginal, broken, and utterly desperate situations of total dependence. It was in these situations where the power of God would be seen. He leaves the wise to their "wisdom" and the elevated to their puffed-up ideas and He moves to places and situations where it will be clear to all Who is responsible for change.

By far, conflicts and divisions in the Church revolve around issues of preference about our man-made methods and programs. We spend all sorts of emotional energy fighting with each other about how we are going to do church services or reach people with the love of Christ, instead of humbling ourselves in positions of complete dependence and calling out to God in prayer. It would be inconsistent with the history of God's interaction with His people for the Holy Spirit to fall upon a divided and arrogant "church" preoccupied with the commercialism of the Kingdom. I've been intimately involved in church leadership for long enough to be convinced that if we spent half as much time and energy in unified, desperate prayer as we do arguing about how to be most effective, we would see God bring about transformation in the lives and communities we exist to serve.

Chapter 8 - So now what?

1. What is the effect of affluence on passionate spirituality?

2. Think of a time when you had an intimate relationship with God. What were the reasons for this closeness?

3. Why do you think that people from "poor" countries often have a more intimate relationship with God?

4. What motivates you to pray?

5. What is it that consumes the majority of your emotional energy and time?

6. Thinking back over the past 10 years in the life of your church, what are the kinds of things or issues that have consumed the majority of people's emotional energy, time, and money?

7. Where in your life do you see a direct connection between the condition of your spiritual life and the degree of your investment in the lives of others?

Chapter 9

Self-Centered Living
vs. Self-Emptying Love

Dying to Self

Our daughter loves to sing. She has always enjoyed music and loves worship songs that are sung in public worship services. Every time we get in the car she wants us to turn on the music. A few years ago, when she was about 6, I caught her in a streak of being really kind to her family and friends and I wanted to encourage what I saw in her young life. I told her how much I loved watching her being kind to people and, when I'd finished, she said to me, "Daddy…it's because I love to sing worship songs." Her simple cause-and-effect statement struck me. I was more focused on the life she was living without realizing what was *creating* that life I was seeing. She explained further, "Whenever I sing worship songs I just feel like being nice to people." She had made the simple yet profound connection between our passion for God and our compassion for those around us. A life lived in intimacy with God produces His reflection. He exchanges our value system for His and thereby changes us into His likeness.

Most leaders today intellectually know there is need in our world and likely believe we should be doing more to meet the need. However, most are paralyzed by the immensity of the need, not knowing where or how to start addressing such massive and complex issues. Our resources and efforts to affect change are eclipsed by a sea of suffering and need. Yet we need to be convinced that if God has given us this mission to be a compassionate Church that could eradicate extreme poverty, He has also given us the spiritual and material resources greater than the need that exists. God's love for His people and His creation would not allow Him to call us to a task that He wouldn't also empower us to fully realize.

The change we seek and that I believe is possible around the globe begins first within the Church. As the popular saying goes, we must be the change we want to see. The most elementary change that must take place on a widespread personal and corporate basis is a sustained move away from the Western norm of self-centered choices and lifestyles toward self-emptying love and compassion. I can't think of any of the multi-faceted and complex factors that cause poverty and social injustice that do not have the same common denominator as the first selfish decision that took place in the Garden of Eden. The root of materialism, consumerism, corruption, and hoarding of resources, from ignorance to needless suffering and all that is broken in our world is the pattern of prioritizing self over others. Simply put, we *want* to use our resources for ourselves more than we *want* to use them for the suffering world.

For those who call themselves followers of Christ and who are being transformed into His likeness, the hallmark of that transformation is a life characterized by self-emptying priorities and choices that declare that others are more important than ourselves. This shift will affect every aspect of personal and corporate life and, unless it does, the transformation we envision will simply be a utopian dream. Even a quick and abbreviated look at the macro statistics of resource distribution and extreme suffering confirms that the Western Church already possesses enough material resources to eradicate needless suffering. The incredibly simple-yet-difficult choice we have is whether or not we are going to prioritize the basic needs of the desperately poor over the materialistic lives defined by comfort and excess of the Western Church today. These are the day-to-day small decisions about how we are going to use our time, treasures, and talents toward a global movement of compassion and justice. We cannot continue to make the same choices, with the same set of priorities and values, and expect people and communities to rise out of poverty.

I believe that there is no more painful yet powerful journey toward the life Christ intended for His people, and consequently a Church He intended for the world, than following Him into death to self. If self-promotion is the root of everything that is unjust, dying to self is the root of everything that leads to life. In the constant struggle to live the life Christ intended is the constant call to follow Him into dying to the never-satisfied monster of self. However, our narcissistic (self-centered) and hedonistic (living for pleasure) default setting causes us to constantly look for ways to preserve, promote, and protect self. This condition is only exacerbated by unprecedented prosperity, and it fosters pride, arrogance, entitlement, materialism, consumerism, and self-sufficiency, all conditions that we read about in Scripture that God came against with determined resolve. Although God has undoubtedly blessed this generation as He has for thousands of years, we have replaced God with the very objects with which He has blessed us. We even consider a life of pleasure and ease as the fruit of God's blessing and favor, a notion that is completely unbiblical and in fact leads to God's condemnation. We think there is something spiritually wrong when we encounter difficulty or anything that causes us to deny ourselves.

In John Piper's book, *Desiring God*, the author accurately writes about the reality that God's gifts are the greatest obstacles to our affection for Him:

The greatest enemy of hunger for God is not poison but apple pie. It is not the banquet of the wicked that dulls our appetite for heaven, but endless nibbling at the table of the world. It is not the X-rated video, but the prime-time dribble of triviality we drink in every night. For all the ill that Satan can do, when God describes what keeps us from the banquet table of his love, it is a piece of land, a yoke of oxen, and a wife (Luke 14:18-20). The greatest adversary of love to God is not his enemies but his gifts. And the most deadly appetites are not for the poison of evil, but for the simple pleasures of earth. For when these replace an appetite for God himself, the idolatry is scarcely recognizable, and almost incurable.[1]

This idolatry is the cancer of our affluent and blessed society. When we think of idolatry, we typically think of worshiping pagan symbols or bowing to images fashioned by human hands; however, the Western Church is just as guilty of the ancient idolatry we read about in the Bible. While we are not usually giving our affection to a carved piece of wood or stone, we are guilty of giving our affection to items manufactured to appeal to our priority for self. In a society addicted to the notion of comfort, ease, and self-gratification, Paul's message from Romans 6 is completely counterintuitive:

Well then, should we keep on sinning so that God can show us more and more of his wonderful grace? Of course not! Since we have died to sin, how can we continue to live in it? Or have you forgotten that when we were joined with Christ Jesus in baptism, we joined him in his death? For we died and were buried with Christ by baptism. And just as Christ was raised from the dead by the glorious power of the Father, now we also may live new lives. Since we have been united with him in his death, we will also be raised to life as he was. We know that our old sinful selves were crucified with Christ so that sin might lose its power in our lives. We are no longer slaves to sin. For when we died with Christ we were set free from the power of sin. And since we died with Christ, we know we will also live with him. We are sure of this because Christ was raised from the dead, and he will never die again. Death no longer has any power over him. When he died, he died once to break the power of sin. But now that he lives, he lives for the glory of God. So you also should consider yourselves to be dead to the power of sin and alive to God through Christ Jesus. Do not let sin control the way you live; do not give in to sinful desires. Do not let any part of your body become an instrument of evil to serve sin. Instead, give yourselves completely to God, for you were dead, but now you have new life. So use your whole body as an instrument to do what is right for the glory of God. Sin is no longer your master, for you no longer live under the requirements of the law. Instead, you live under the freedom of God's grace….when you were slaves to sin, you were free from the obligation to do right. And what was the result? You are now ashamed of the things you used to do, things that end in eternal doom. But now you are free from the power of sin and have become slaves of God. Now you do those things that lead to holiness and result in eternal life. (Romans 6:1-14, 20-22)

A dead slave can do nothing at all in service to the master, and those who have entered into a relationship with Christ live in a positional reality of being dead to sin. Before a relationship with Christ, we don't have the ability or the power to live a life that reflects Christ: we are enslaved to the power of sin and its self-centered decisions and choices. Our identification and representation is with Adam and his decision to prioritize self and open the door to self-centered living. Adam's choice to be like God (Gen 3:1-6), to put himself at the center of his universe, started humankind down the road to hedonism that has been enabled by access to unprecedented wealth. Adam's choice to sin initiated our inability to prioritize the needs of others over our own selfish desires.

Praise God that this choice was not the end of the story! Our relationship with Christ gives us new identification, representation, and ability. Our unity with Christ starts with our dying with Him. Our old self is crucified along with Christ and our new self is raised with Him. The practice of this great theological truth means that we live with the possibility that we can always choose to die to self in our moment-by-moment decisions. We can access the power necessary to constantly prioritize the needs of others over the self-centered desires that can otherwise win out over a life of simplicity, service, and generosity. We are empowered to place God and His compassionate priorities at the center of our universe.

As the worship song is sung:

> *When I survey the wondrous cross*
> *On which the Prince of Glory died*
> *My richest gain I count but loss*
> *And pour contempt on all my pride.*
>
> *See from His head, His hands, His feet*
> *Sorrow and love flow mingled down*
> *Did ever such love and sorrow meet*
> *Or thorns compose so rich a crown?*
>
> *O the wonderful cross, O the wonderful cross*
> *Bids me come and die and find that I may truly live*
> *O the wonderful cross, O the wonderful cross*
> *All who gather here by grace draw near and bless*
> *Your name!*

Were the whole realm of nature mine
That were an offering far too small
Love so amazing, so divine
Demands my soul, my life, my all.[2]

However, as promising and empowering as that truth sounds, dying to self involves the same unavoidable pain, sacrifice and self-denial as physical death. The inherent discomfort of self-denial violently confronts our culture's priorities for pleasure, comfort, and ease. We must accept that living this way of life will include a revolutionary and radical abandonment of these cultural values. If we choose to follow Christ to the cross we will be clearly identified as "not of this world." We must also accept the fact that the change we seek will not happen without pain, sacrifice, and self-denial. We cannot hold in one hand the values of this world and in the other the values of a self-denying passion for the poor. People and communities who have accomplished great things for the Kingdom have done so with considerable sacrifice and personal cost. How can we expect a contemporary revolution of compassion without the same cost?

More than a positional reality of being dead to self, we are also given an example of how to live out the daily experiences of self-emptying love that changes our lives and the lives of those around us. In this day of self-preservation, promotion, and protection, listen to these descriptions of the opposite. Within the context of living a life that is patterned after Christ's, I refer again to Paul's letter to the Philippians:

> Do nothing out of selfish ambition or vain concept, but in humility consider others better than yourselves. Each of you should look not only to your own interests, but also to the interests of others. Your attitude should be the same as that of Christ Jesus. Who, being in very nature God, did not consider equality with God something to be grasped, but made himself nothing, taking the very nature of a servant, being made in human likeness. And being found in appearance of man, he humbled himself and became obedient to death on a cross. (Phil 2:3-8, NIV)

Can you imagine what would happen if God's people, en masse, lived out this instruction? Can you imagine the world changing potential if Christ followers everywhere "emptied themselves" and lived out a global chorus of compassion? Read it again in another version:

> Don't be selfish; don't try to impress others. Be humble, thinking of others better than yourselves. Don't look out only for your own interests, but take an interest in others too. You must have the same attitude that Christ Jesus had. Though he was God, he did not think equality with God as something to cling to. Instead, he gave up his divine privileges; he took the humble position of a slave

and was born as a human being. When he appeared in human form, he humbled himself in obedience to God and died a criminal's death on a cross. (Phil 2:3-8 NLT)

Lives constantly committed to self-emptying love will affect every corner of our existence. Christ-like self-emptying love will transform our marriages, our children, our work places, our churches, and our communities. It will affect every relationship positively.

Examining the implications of living self-emptying love would consume volumes of writing. However, I want to look specifically at how self-emptying living must affect core changes to the resources of our faith communities, time, and money if we are ever to realize a Church that could affect the kind of global change necessary to eradicate needless suffering.

Church and Dying to Self

We have already looked at enough convincing evidence of the general failure of the Western Church to live up to its intended potential and the reasons it no longer has a credible voice. My intent here is not to repeat myself. I do, however, want to address how we as individuals who make up the Church have brought our self-centered priorities into the Church and how that has affected our mission in the world.

In the second half of the last century, as affluence and the resulting comforts and choices became a cultural norm, our expectations of church were swept up in a wave of consumerism. As we had more choices at the grocery store we expected more choices at church. As we had the ability to have tailor-made suits and custom golf clubs, we expected personalized programming on Sunday mornings. The proliferation of musical tastes and genres caused a proliferation of music styles and expectations. As marketing and advertising strategically appealed to our newfound ability for comfort and entertainment, we expected church to be comfortable and pastors to be entertaining. Do you think our ability to have a Lazyboy in our homes might have had something to do with replacing the wooden pews with padded ones?

This self-absorbed shift in priority has had a commensurate effect on what consumes the Church's resources of time, leadership, money, and emotional and spiritual energy. When our individual question for the Church is, "What will the Church do for me?" instead of, "What can I do for the Church?" we have made a subtle but crippling shift. After a few years of church ministry, I stopped and evaluated my impact and that of the programs in the church I was responsible for. I was fully under the weight of expectations from those inside the church who felt that it was my job to create the preferential environment that would keep them happy, attending, and giving. At one time, I looked at my appointment book and was shocked to realize that the majority of my time was going to:

- Meeting with parents, who told me the kinds of events that would keep their kids' attention and therefore secure their support of my leadership.

- Meeting with young adults to design a program that would meet their social needs and keep them from going to the church down the road.

- Meeting with musicians to hear about why we should try to sound like the latest album.

- Meeting with older folks to hear why we should keep doing what we did 30 years ago.

- Meeting with people who were too afraid to tell other pastors directly what they weren't doing right.

- Meeting with church leaders who were constantly frustrated by what was perceived as the non-committal attitude of people within their church.

My heart, mind, and spirit were consumed with the mission of trying to meet the expectations of those who thought we could be a "church for everyone." This is a catchy way of saying the leaders are working their hardest to try to please everyone. Hearing words like, "I'm not being fed" is the most obvious and honorable sounding way of saying, "They are not listening to me or doing things my way." Our most deeply held personal values can become expectations for what everyone else should value. As a result, our individual preferences for church activities and programs become traditions and these traditions become sacred. Anyone who has been in church or church leadership for any length of time can think of examples of preferences that have become sacred. Talking with some people about the way we do communion is just as touchy as talking about getting rid of communion altogether. Talking with some people about the effectiveness of Sunday School is just as sensitive as a discussion about the divinity of Jesus. When our preferences become sacred, we keep adding new programs to church life without ever questioning the effectiveness and validity of old programs.

Think about the effect this has on what we use our money for. A salaried pastor for each age demographic, facilities, and décor that will meet the "needs" of as many groups as possible; supplies, materials, and equipment that will capture and keep the attention of whomever is listening; conferences and training that will help you be like the latest mega-church you're being compared to. All of this to meet the expectations of those who are already on the inside!

We have lost our mission to transform the world around us and replaced it with the mission of trying not to lose those we already have. I am not saying that churches don't value outreach or missions. We know we should value those things, but as leaders, we often place more value on job security and the approval of people.

I grew up thinking that the enemies of the biblical mission of the Church were the likes of secular humanism, atheism, pluralism, relativism, agnosticism, and political correctness. I was wrong. The real enemies of the Church's mission are its entitled and self-interested members and the leaders who spend their existence enabling and validating the idea that the purpose of the Church is to cater to those members' spiritual preferences. This enemy is much more subtle and therefore more dangerous.

The Church does not exist to serve itself: it exists to serve the world. However, the Church in North America is currently mired in issues of style and preference. Not until the individuals who make up the Church choose to follow Christ in death to our preferences, style, rights, and traditions will we become a Church that could impact a world that is desperate for transformation. The world is hungry for the Church to serve as Christ intended, but we will never become agents of change until we deal with and die to self as it relates to our personal expectations of the Church. In his book, *The Unstoppable Force*, Erwin McManus makes the powerful connection between self-emptying service and the Church's power for transformation:

> The purpose of the church cannot be to survive or even to thrive but to serve. And sometimes servants die in serving...the church is not called to survive history but to serve humanity. The life of the church is the heart of God. The heart of God is to serve a broken world. When

Jesus wrapped a towel around his waist, he reminded us that only he could wash away our sin. The church cannot live when the heart of God is not beating within her. God's heartbeat is to seek and save that which is lost. The church exists to serve as the body of Christ, and it's through this commitment to serve that we are forced to engage our culture. The serving we are called to requires direct contact. You cannot wash the feet of a dirty world if you refuse to touch it. There is a sense of mystery to this, but it is in serving that the church finds her strength... When the church refuses to serve the world, she begins to waste away...Following Jesus is a dangerous undertaking. He was willing to die on our behalf. The Father was not only willing to let himself die, but he commanded it. The only way that I could truly follow God was to die to myself and live for him. Only dead men can follow the God of the Cross.[3]

What is your attitude and expectation of your local church and its leadership? Are you currently frustrated by what you perceive as the leadership not "listening" to you? Would those close to you say that you have developed a critical and judgmental spirit toward your church and its leadership? How much emotional time and energy are you spending trying to change your church or its programs to meet your needs or fulfill your preferential expectations? Are you constantly disappointed that the church isn't feeding you spiritually? If any of these questions describes your general attitude toward your local body of believers, you are, in all likelihood, further crippling the achievement of the Church's true mission. You have likely placed your desires before the needs of the desolate world the Church exists to serve.

If your true desire is to be used of God as part of a local church to transform lives next door and around the world, follow Christ to the cross and die to yourself. Pick up a towel and serve someone.

Money and Dying to Self

We can't talk about a vision of a world transformed and a Church that leads the way without dealing with the issue of money. It costs money, and a lot of it, to make the kind of investments that will bring about transformation in lives and communities all around the world. No matter how much we may want to avoid or soft-peddle the issue, we must deal directly and boldly with how we use the financial resources with which we have been entrusted.

I want to say up front that money is not inherently evil or wrong, nor is it wrong to have a lot of it. It is not wrong to enjoy what material wealth brings. The reality is that many servants of God in Scripture were rewarded materially for their faithfulness and obedience. Abraham, Job, David, and Solomon are just the first who come to mind who, as a direct result of their faithfulness, are notable for being blessed with material wealth. Abraham, when he was called by God to leave his home, took his wealth with him (Genesis 12:6). It was Job's riches that became part of God's test for him and, as a result of his faithfulness, he was given twice as much wealth as he had before the trial (Job 42:10). Known as the greatest King of Israel and a man after God's heart, David was described as *"having enjoyed a long life, wealth, and honor"* (1 Chronicles 29:28). Solomon asked God for wisdom, not for his own benefit but for the benefit of those he led, and God specifically responded by telling him that he would be rewarded with *"wealth, riches and fame such as no other king has had before or will have in the future"* (2 Chronicles 1:12). At the end of his life and reign, there was an exhaustive description of his unprecedented wealth, fulfilling God's promise (2 Chronicles 9:13-28). Clearly, material prosperity is a gift from God, and possessing wealth, even by global standards, is not, in and of itself, evil or sinful. Unfortunately, many in the relief and development community, for the purpose of fundraising, engage in guilt-motivated tactics, conveying that it is wrong to posses wealth relative to the world's poor.

Such a fundraising strategy typically results in short-term token giving at best, but more often, it simply turns off those who truly want to invest in changing lives. People are tired of images on the TV showing the faces of dirty, starving children in Africa. Fundraisers from the relief and development community underestimate the fact that people, given an opportunity and motivated by vision of change, will invest far more than the cost of a monthly sponsorship. While God is using the funds generated this way to impact lives all around the world, this type of giving and generosity is a drop in the proverbial bucket held up against the biblical vision of generosity and compared to the degree of resource imbalance that exists in our world.

As I write this, I am sitting in a small house in rural Uganda, spending some time with one of our excellent partner organizations that is caring for abandoned and orphaned children and is engaged in fantastic community development work. I am here with a church team from Canada which has partnered to build a vocational high school for the children from the orphan home and surrounding community. Just a couple of days ago, Peter, the local leader, received a call from the local police station asking us to come and pick up another child. Peter, another member of the team, and I, went out to the police station and were taken into a small metal round room with a dirt floor. At first we didn't see him but behind the desk sat a little boy wearing only a filthy t-shirt. He was sitting in the dirt, lethargic with obvious signs of neglect and malnutrition. His skin felt like leather, dehydrated from not being provided enough to eat or drink. His only movement was to scratch his body, covered in sores that were from either ant or mosquito bites. His little belly was distended, another obvious sign of hunger and starvation. His ear was pierced with a small stick, presumably to mark him "imperfect." Apparently, this was done to protect him from becoming a child sacrifice if he was found by a traditional animist.

He looked about eight months old but nothing was known about him: not his birthday or even his name. He was found by a street cop, abandoned, sitting on the side of the road. The officer picked him up and brought him to the police station. They kept him there, sitting on the floor for a week, hoping that someone would change their mind and come looking for him. When that seemed unlikely, they called Peter and asked if he would come and take him back to the children's home. I held him for the drive back. He was too weak to make the smallest noise and could barely hold his head up.

Once he got back to the children's home he was washed, given clean clothes, and fed a bottle of milk. His hunger caused him to make short work of ten ounces of milk. Within just hours, he was already showing a marked response to these simple demonstrations of love. He had perked up and was even smiling. It has been a few days now and tonight I fed him a plate of mashed potatoes. Between bites he laid his head down on his crossed little arms that rested on the high chair tray as if to communicate that he was still weary from the suffering of the past number of months. Within just a few hours, this little fighter went from being tossed out like yesterday's garbage to receiving all the basics that every child should have: clean clothes, shelter, food and affection from those who are willing to treat him as their own.

But here is the simple reality: it cost money to transform this little life. Were it not for the generous supporters of Peter and his work in Uganda, this little life would likely have ended.

The most reoccurring theme in the teachings of Jesus was about the Kingdom of God. He was here to announce and demonstrate God's way of life and living. Next to the Kingdom, Jesus spoke most often about money and its use, communicating that the issues surrounding wealth are the biggest obstacles to living out God's Kingdom on Earth. Jesus lays it out in an early teaching to His followers:

> Don't store up treasures for yourself here on earth, where moths eat them and rust destroys them, and where thieves break in and steal. Store your treasures in heaven, where moths and rust cannot destroy, and thieves do not break in and steal. **Wherever your treasure is, there the desires of our heart will also be.** (Matthew 6:19-21, emphasis added))

If you really want to measure the condition of your heart, priorities and values, then simply take a look at your bank statements and receipts. According to Jesus, what we do with our money is a window into our soul's condition, an audit of our spiritual health. This being the case, I want to look again at a few of the Western macro spending realities I presented in Part One:

- World golf spending: $40 billion[4]

- Dieting programs in the US: $40 billion[5]

- Online pornography revenue worldwide in 2006: $97 billion[6]

- Cosmetics in the US: $8 billion[7]

- Ice Cream in Europe: $11 billion[8]

- Perfume in Europe and the US: $12 billion[9]

- Cigarettes in Europe: $50 billion[10]

- Real estate owned by institutional churches in the US: $230 billion[11]

- Given to church buildings per year by Christians: $9 - $11 billion[12]

Again, realizing that an investment of $40 billion a year would eradicate extreme suffering, the striking truth revealed by the imbalance in these numbers tells us that, as a whole, we value our appearance, buildings, smoking, and luxury items grossly more than 27,000 children dying every day from easily preventable causes. Corporately, Western Christians could erase the extreme and unnecessary suffering of one billion people in this lifetime without ever really sacrificing or putting ourselves in any kind of economic peril. We might have to give up the excessive comforts and luxuries we have come to pretend are necessities, but we don't need to truly sacrifice.

While this message is primarily targeted at those who would consider themselves insiders of the Church, ending extreme poverty is even more possible if we look to engage the multitudes of those outside of the Church who are motivated more by humanitarian values than spiritual ones. The resources outside of the Western Church and society's growing concern for issues of justice and compassion present opportunities for greater global leadership by the Church and promise of a world transformed. Corporate social responsibility, high-profile, massive philanthropic donations, bold declarations, prophetic speeches by politicians, activists and celebrities, all in the current environment of globalization, have significantly raised the sense of awareness of the crisis and the urgency to address it.

In 2000, world leaders committed to the following Millennium Development Goals (MDGs) before the United Nations:

- Goal 1: Eradicate Extreme Poverty and Hunger

- Goal 2: Achieve Universal Primary Education

- Goal 3: Promote Gender Equality and Empower Women

- Goal 4: Reduce Child Mortality

- Goal 5: Improve Maternal Health

- Goal 6: Combat HIV/AIDS, Malaria and Other Diseases

- Goal 7: Ensure Environmental Sustainability

- Goal 8: Develop a Global Partnership For Development

The obstacles and complexities of ending extreme poverty are many, and more than financial investments and interventions are needed to holistically and sustainably assist developing nations; however, money is essential and arguably the most difficult ingredient to access. Jeffrey Sachs, the macroeconomist who was the special advisor to the former Secretary-General of the United Nations, Kofi Annan, asserts that additional financial targets are necessary if we hope to meet these aggressive goals to eradicate extreme suffering. He asserts that an additional investment of $48 billion was needed for 2006 and $74 billion for 2015.[13]

Looking beyond the Church, we know that if everyone from officially developed countries gave only $200 per year to end extreme poverty, it would total roughly $171 billion dollars: more than enough to get the job done.[14] Peter Singer proposes that if people from developed countries gave only 5% of their personal income, it would also add up to more than enough money to meet the Millennium Development Goals.[16] Collectively, we could quite easily give at levels needed to provide the basic necessities of life for everyone on the planet without putting ourselves in any real jeopardy. With almost a billion people today suffering under extreme poverty, we are all complicit in one of history's greatest disasters.

Having said that, I also want to warn those of us who feel passionate about injustice and poverty. We would be wrong to prescribe a lifestyle and personal choices for other followers of Christ. In our zeal and commitment for change, we can easily find ourselves trying to play the role of the Holy Spirit and become just as legalistic as the religious police we read about earlier. Can we golf, eat ice cream, go on vacations, build nice homes and churches and still live self-emptying and generous towards the poor? Of course! God never condemned money or wealth. He condemned the *love* of money and a wealth that ignored the poor.

What these numbers reveal is that there exists an immense imbalance. The degree to which global resources are disproportionately distributed is itself, a convicting reality; it should cause all of us to examine where we allocate our personal resources and ask the hard questions about priorities and values. These figures are a wide open window, revealing the spiritual corrosion in the Western followers of Jesus. The appropriate response is personal and corporate repentance, followed by drastic moves toward humble generosity and simplicity.

In our highly individualistic and privatized Western society, we have overly privatized the role that money plays in our spiritual lives. Christian leaders are often extremely timid and hesitant to speak directly and boldly to issues of personal and corporate resource use and, as a result, we are both missing a key element to the spiritual health we all seek and crippling the global advancement of God's Kingdom. We eagerly preach about the importance of the Great Commission and the greatest commandments, but stop short of a courageous call to a discipleship that impacts our wallets. Church leaders are typically scheduled or slotted to speak about the issue of money whenever the church falls behind financially, as if the issue was a "user pays" motivation for giving our money. If we reduce the topic of resource use to this, we are missing the whole point that what we do with our money is just as much a matter of worship as the songs we sing in our gatherings.

Writing about the role of finances and compassion in the Church's mission, John Rowell states:

> Because missions and money are inseparable concerns, we must make sure they remain married in our minds so that we do not miss the mark the Spirit of God calls us to aim for as Christian witnesses. If we are to take the gospel of the kingdom of God to those who are poor, our missiology must have significant theology of stewardship (including a decidedly financial factor) woven into its fabric.[17]

There is no way around the issue that a vision of a Church that changes the world must assign a high value to boldly challenging Western believers to revolutionize how we view and use "our" money. On the whole, we generally act like our money is ours; however, we must gain a deep-rooted understanding that all we have comes from and belongs to God, whether it comes from a hard-earned paycheck, a birthday gift, or an inheritance. When the issue of ultimate ownership is confused, the decisions on how to use resources are easily turned toward self-centered priorities. Whether or not we generously worship with our finances will be the litmus test of true allegiance to Christ and a factor that can limit us in reflecting His likeness. Clearly, the Western Church is worshipping the god of money and materialism right along with the rest of modern society. If our heart's affection is for money and possessions, the most powerful act of repentance from this idolatry is to give generously to those who need it more than we do.

Our primary motivation to give shouldn't be to respond to need or because people need it more than we do: it should be to worship our Father. It should first have everything to do with the health of our spiritual lives. We should give out of a joy that realizes that everything we have comes from God, not just 10%. However, we also don't have the luxury of waiting to give generously until we *feel* like giving. The condition of our spiritual health *should* create a joy of generosity; however, authentic discipleship *would* result in faithful obedience regarding resource distribution, which *could* result in social justice that reflects the person of Jesus. In his most often quoted work on the topic, Ron Sider challenges his readers to:

> Imagine what one quarter of the world's Christians could do if they became truly generous. A few of us could move to desperately poor areas...The rest of us could defy surrounding materialism. We could refuse to let our affluent would squeeze us into its consumeristic mold. Instead, we could become generous nonconformists who love Jesus more than wealth. In obedience to our Lord, we could empower the poor through small loans, community development, and better societal systems. And in the process we would learn again His paradoxical truth that true happiness flows from generosity.[18]

We are simply without excuse. The money is there, but the will to affect historical and global change hasn't been. Nonetheless, those who have had their hearts broken by global injustice, while beyond frustrated by the affluence of the Western Church, can't help but hope that everything can and must change. They hold in one hand the needless and extreme suffering of a billion people, on the other hand, a Church that, if we truly lived like Jesus, could absolutely change this world.

However, we will have to redefine generosity in a way that stands out from current common giving practices. Putting what we can afford, or dumping our "extra" money in the offering plate is normal; giving beyond our means is generous. Putting a few coins in the Salvation Army kettle at Christmas is common; providing a whole meal and gifts for a family in need is generous. Sponsoring a child in a developing country is common; sponsoring as many as you can is generous. Giving a few cans to the food bank is common; spending regular time serving in a homeless shelter is generous. Giving $50 to the latest disaster is common; going without an exotic vacation so you can travel to serve in a disaster zone is generous.

I challenge you to track your spending for six months. Keep track of everything you spend your money on to see where your heart really is. Then ask yourself if you are common or generous. Ask yourself if your use of money reflects your *needs* or your *wants*. Have the courage to see what you would be able to give away if you became simply obedient and what more you could give if you became truly generous.

Time and Dying to Self

While money has the potential to achieve great things, we must not forget about a resource that can be of even more life-changing and tangible value. Never before in history has a civilization been so experienced, educated, trained, or specialized. The Western world, and now much of the developing world, contains huge amounts of knowledge and expertise. Putting aside financial inputs and ability, we also possess more than enough knowledge and skill to solve most of the complex technical issues that contribute to the creation and perpetuation of poverty. The immense global imbalance of knowledge and expertise, although not measurable, is likely greater than the global imbalance of financial resources.

Jeffrey Sachs proposes that if the most desperately poor countries had access to what he calls the "Big Five" we could eradicate needless absolute poverty. If the least developed nations could have access to the following, the world would be transformed:[19]

1. clean water and sanitation;

2. education;

3. health care;

4. agriculture;

5. basic infrastructure of power, transportation, and communication.

Read the list again.

The knowledge and skills needed to assist the poorest countries to gain access to these five basic building blocks are miniscule compared to the vast knowledge base that exists in the world. Rapid advances in technology, science, space exploration, health care, human services, environmental protection, business, leadership, and management tower in comparison to the knowledge base needed to eradicate needless suffering in only a generation. As with material wealth, the available resources of knowledge and experience far exceed the degree of need that exists. The idea that the average westerner is unable to do anything to address the complex global issues of poverty is a demonic lie that keeps the hearts of the affluent lukewarm, and keeps the lives of the poor buried under the despondency of hopelessness.

I have seen the lives of both Canadian grandmothers and African orphans changed by what they have to give to each other: time. I have seen the lives of extremely wealthy business people and desperately poor villagers changed because of what they have to give to each other: time. The West is now entering into a period of a grossly overpopulated and underutilized generation that has never been more trained and experienced. Baby boomers are retiring, having amassed a tremendous amount of money and realizing a tremendous amount of free time. And while I hear over and over again that boomers are looking forward to enjoying the freedom of their retirement, the very next words I hear go something like this, "I'm looking forward to sitting by the pool and golfing a bit more, but I also don't want to do that for 12 months of the year. I want to use my resources to serve God and to make a difference."

What incredible world changing potential! Imagine an entire generation, with the kind of knowledge, experience, and skill that saw rapid industrialization and extreme wealth, being focused and utilized to provide access to the basics of life for the poorest of the planet; it leaves me with the hope that this dream can be realized faster than we think. Without minimizing the human factor and leadership development that must take place in the developing world, a world without needless suffering is completely possible.

The generation after the boomers is also emerging with a very different set of values than their parents and grandparents. It is a generation that is passionate about compassion, realizing that enormous affluence has not brought the joy and fulfillment it promised. In fact, it is a generation disillusioned and disappointed by a lack of relational substance from their parents and grandparents who worked so hard to give their children a "better life," as defined by material wealth. Their disappointment, in many cases, is being channeled to living out a very different existence than one defined by comfort, safety, and security. They are giving up vacations for volunteering and luxury for real life. They are realizing that real joy and fulfillment is found in giving, not in receiving.

This time and the willingness to invest it in others, combined with remarkable financial resources, means the world is primed for a significant move toward a historical generosity; we could soon witness a new age of compassion that remarkably resembles the original design of the Church as described in Acts, "...*there were no needy people among them, because those who owned land or houses would sell them and bring the money to the apostles to give to those in need*" (4:34-35). Ron Sider also calls us to worship with our time as well as with our money, "If you preach the gospel in all aspects with the exception of the issues which deal specifically with your time you are not preaching the gospel at all."[19]

For many, time is more precious than money. They have much more money than they have time, and it's easier to cut a large check and remain divorced from a life of compassion. We often hear the adage that God wants more than your pocketbook: He wants your life. And there are some that avoid the personal sacrifice of direct involvement by giving great amounts of money. Their challenge to move toward a life of compassion is to surrender and worship with their time: to donate their scarce amount of time to serve the least in this world. They will find that, through service, *their* lives are enriched far more than they will enrich the lives of others.

Borrowing from Matthew and Isaiah, and consistent with the way God worked out His mission throughout Scripture and church history, "Go and spend yourself" is the call of God upon

His church. The world's most challenging, complex, and painful realities are beckoning the followers of Jesus to go and spend ourselves. Just as Jesus came and spent Himself on our behalf, so we are invited to partner with Him to do the same. Stop and think for a moment where you can go and spend yourself. It might be as simple and obvious as:

- sending an email to someone who might be discouraged or defeated

- writing a card to a family member who wouldn't expect it

- walking across the street to say hello to the people who just moved in

- having people over for a meal

Or, it could be as extensive as:

- moving specifically to a lower income neighborhood to care for those with practical needs

- saying no to a higher paying job or transfer to continue to build into relationships that need the presence of Christ

- spending two weeks (and a chunk of money) each year to care for children orphaned by AIDS in Africa

- moving your family to the other side of the world to live among and serve the poorest of the poor

The mission of God, simply put, is to visibly and tangibly bring about His Kingdom to His creation. And while I sometimes wonder about the wisdom of God's tactic, He has chosen us, His followers, as the primary method to accomplish the coming of this Kingdom. Going and spending ourselves is the only way that the dominion of God will be evidenced in this world that so desperately needs the evidence. The proof of God's Kingdom is power, joy, compassion, justice, mercy, peace, and love. None of this happens without going and spending ourselves.

Toward Simplicity

The monumental shift in how we value time and money will never happen if we continue to think that we can give out of our excess. To think that we can impact the world by giving our leftover money or our left over time is foolishness. In our self-centered value system, we will never have enough money and time to give away. This kind of change won't come from sharper marketing or communication techniques. It will only come when followers of Jesus commit to living out their life in a contemporary life of simplicity. Following the ancient but completely relevant wisdom of the Proverbs:

Oh God, I beg two favors from you; let me have them before I die. First, help me to never tell a lie. Second, give me neither poverty nor riches! Give me just enough to satisfy my needs. For if I grow rich, I may deny you and say, "Who is this

Lord?" And if I am poor, I may steal and thus insult God's holy name. (Proverbs 30:7-9)

Within the context of a grossly affluent Western Church and a grossly suffering world, this prayer should be always on our lips. In fact, we should have been praying it long ago. If our personal and corporate repentance doesn't lead us toward simpler lives that enable us to share what we have, we may be sorry, but we are not repentant.

I believe that each of us needs to seek God for specifically how we should now live. After looking at the injustice of the global imbalance of resources and the biblical picture of a compassionate church, would it be too much to...

- Think about selling our homes and moving into smaller homes or shared living to enable us to free up resources

- Seriously figure how much we absolutely need to live on and to give the rest away

- Share items with other believers or neighbors to reduce the amount we need to individually own

- Reduce the gifts we give to each other on special occasions

- Figure out how to live with one car or share transportation where it is possible

- Sell our church building to use the funds for community development in poor countries and share the use of other church facilities with other congregations or community centers

- Liquidate excess assets or land and give away the money that is generated

- Regularly plan on traveling to personally participate in relief of suffering and community development, building a relationship with your new global neighbors

And the list could go on and on, limited only by our imagination and propensity toward self or selflessness.

Now is a good time to warn those who are passionate and dialed into generosity enabled by a lifestyle of simplicity. The specifics of how to make the desire for a life of simplicity and generosity "hit the ground" and start to make a difference will be extremely varied. It is dangerous ground for those of us with unquenched zeal for justice and compassion to begin to prescribe what a compassionate Christian life looks like for others. To spend our time looking for some nebulous "line" or formula that tells us what we are allowed to spend our time and money on, and still live a self-emptying sacrificial life, will result in the same judgmental and critical pharisaical spirit that we rail against the religious leaders for. To ask whether or not we can participate in certain activities or whether or not we can buy *this* or spend our time on *that* completely misses the point. The core question to ask ourselves and to ask each other is, "Are we increasingly moving toward a life of simplicity and sacrificial generosity that puts a greater value on the needs of others than my comfort or security?" We are a long way from basic obedience when it comes to possessions and giving, and we're nowhere near sacrificial. We cannot presume we know what that means for everyone in every situation. Christians typically jump in the ditch on one side or another on the issues we are discussing. Some of us look for excuses to get away with giving as little as we possibly can to alleviate our consciences and still be able to call ourselves Christians; others become sacrificially generous and then judge and condemn others for not living the same way we do. Throughout history, social activists and spiritual zealots have developed a narrowly-defined Christian experience and lifestyle that quickly morphs into a self-righteous attitude. As I heard someone say recently, "We need to keep the narrow road as wide as possible."

I am also not suggesting that international development can be as mechanized and formulated as much as those from the developed world would like or expect. Money plus time, stemming from a life of simplicity, doesn't automatically equal development. A movement to eradicate needless suffering flows out of renovated values and priorities. It starts with significant decisions and actions, first by Christian leaders and then their followers, that produce a life of simplicity. And it is to leaders, and their role in this vision, that we now turn our attention and focus.

Chapter 9 - So now what?

1. Give some practical examples of how you, or someone you know, have "died to self" and, in doing so, demonstrated a Christ-like character.

2. In a few words, how would you describe "dying to self" to someone who has never heard that phrase?

3. What is the role of "self" in the decisions you make regarding generosity?

4. Where have you seen the destructive effects of "self" in the ministry of a church you are familiar with?

5. Where do you need to "die to self" when it comes to your expectations of your church and its leaders?

6. Where do you need to "die to self" in matters related to money?

7. Where do you need to "die to self" in matters related to time?

8. What specific ways can you and your family move toward lives of simplicity to enable you to invest more in the lives of the poor?

Chapter 10

The First Steps of Leadership

You First

A discussion about transformational change in the Church that precipitates transformational change in the poorest places of the world is not complete without addressing leaders and their role in the movement. People follow leaders. It is unrealistic and even naïve to assume that the kind of revolution we speak about is possible without having a strong example set by people who have the responsibility to lead God's people. If we expect spiritual and social change in the people of God, we must first expect an even more comprehensive spiritual and social change from those who lead them. We can't even think about preaching and teaching about spiritual transformation and social justice without first being willing to submit ourselves to the sacrifices and costs of this change. This message, if not backed up by real, living examples of the difference we preach, will be vehemently rejected, as, in time, will our leadership. Earlier, we looked at the potentially powerful role that leaders play in articulating and holding a vision before those they lead. The world and this generation of spiritual and social skeptics are desperate for a message of hope and transformation. They are yearning to find substance in amongst the religious and material form; and they are looking for this substance to alter the reality of their lives and the lives of those who suffer needlessly. The warning call, though, is that articulating the hope and anticipation of change will not be sufficient to create the revolution.

This change will cost leaders even more than followers. The sacrifice required to lead many mini-movements of spiritual transformation and compassion will be greater than the sacrifice of those who are led; unless this revolution is first *exemplified*, it will simply turn into the rhetoric of religious fads and book covers. It must be *leaders* who set the example, providing a model of self-emptying love and compassion that leaves behind the cultural shrines of comfort, security, and safety. However, leaders are often susceptible to the lure of self-promotion and a culture of entitlement that people so easily fall into. Leaders had better not preach against consumerism and materialism unless they are making serious steps toward simplicity. They had better not teach about the lure of possessions and money unless they are living lives of modesty. We had better not be challenging people to give generously of their time while we protect our own. The hypocrisy is obvious, usually to everyone but the leader, when from our platforms we preach about prayer, filling of the Holy Spirit, commitment, and sacrifice of our time and money, but during the rest of the week our lives mirror our culture's priorities and not Christ's. Risking overstatement, I strongly believe that the Church lacks moral and social authority mainly because its leaders are not models and examples of Christ-like morality and social priorities. How can we expect people to live out a reality and an ideal that has not been modeled?

I constantly hear leaders complaining about disappointment in their followers. In their frustration, it is common for positional leaders to cast the blame on apparent mediocrity or apathy in the people they lead. However, in their criticism I can also hear and see why followers, or the general Western "Christian" public, are not living out their potential as Spirit-filled agents of change and unusual compassion. Very simply, the people cannot and will not go to a place they have not seen their leaders go. If a critique can be leveled against the people, an even greater indictment is prepared for their leaders. I don't know of an unwanted situation, conflict, or state of affairs that doesn't have its origins somewhere on the continuum between apathetic and completely narcissistic leadership. While I am the last to foster the all-too-common expectation that leaders be perfect, pragmatically speaking, followers are just that – followers. Followers will follow the most compelling and convincing of leaders. Since Machiavelli's *The Prince*, countless people have written, spoken, pontificated, consulted, and taught about leadership. Like no other generation before, influencers have, at the click of a mouse, libraries of information and material about effective and affective leadership and leadership tools. In amongst all that can be read or said about leadership, the terrifying simplicity is that leaders are always the most responsible for the condition a group of people find themselves in.

Christian Leaders Going to Hell

I am absolutely convinced that if the Western Church is spiritually bankrupt and void of power and influence, that very fact would suggest that its leaders are spiritually bankrupt and void of power and influence. I am just as convinced that if the Western Church is characterized by safety, security, and comfort rather than sacrificial, risk-taking faith, Christian leaders are exemplifying that same condition. *And*, if the Western Church is known to value consumerism and materialism over revolutionary compassion, its leaders are just as committed to those same values and ensuing behaviors. Of course there are leaders who are prophetic voices, calling out for and living real transformation in the wilderness of rampant, self-centered norms and decisions. However, the degree of our slumber and apathy is evidence that these voices are still too few. The Western Church has already been long and convincingly led with Western society's values and priorities, an approach which has catastrophically resulted in irrelevance at best. More realistically, our cowardly acceptance of cultural norms has made us complicit in the global imbalance of resources and extreme, unnecessary suffering.

The following are excerpts from a sharply pointed article written by Ron Sider to Christian leaders:

> There is strong biblical reason for thinking that many evangelical leaders are idolatrous heretics. If that statement seems a bit strong, ask yourself these questions: Do today's evangelical leaders come even close to preaching and teaching about God's concern for the poor the way the Bible does? What does the Bible say about those who neglect the poor? And about those who fail to teach their people what God tells them to say?
>
> Three sets of facts simply do not fit together. There is widespread poverty in our world. The Bible says God and his faithful people have a special concern for the poor. And North American Christians give less and less every year. The Bible is full of texts demanding that God's people share God's concern for the poor. Jesus said bluntly that those who neglect the poor will go to hell. "Depart from me, you who are cursed, into the eternal fire prepared for

the devil and his angels. For I was hungry and you gave me nothing to eat" (Matthew 25:41).

If Jesus meant what he said, does not the widespread neglect of the poor in the…church mean we are in danger of eternal damnation? We have vastly more material abundance but, inversely; give less to the work of the kingdom. Mammon is winning the battle for most Christian hearts. Obviously, our Christian leaders -- pastors, Sunday school teachers, seminary professors, and popular speakers -- are guilty of colossal failure.

According to the Bible, leaders are placed as 'watchmen' over God's people: if leaders issue God's warning and the people ignore it, the people are held responsible. But if the leaders fail to warn the people, then God holds the leaders accountable. "When I say to a wicked man, 'You will surely die,' and you do not warn him or speak out to dissuade him from his evil ways in order to save his life, that wicked man will die for his sin, and I will hold you accountable for his blood." (Ezekiel 3:18)

Would anybody claim that evangelical leaders today are talking as much about God's concern for the poor as the Bible does? Would anyone deny that this is the second most common theme in the Bible? If evangelical pastors reviewed their sermons, if evangelical congregations reviewed their educational curricula and total congregational spending, if para-church leaders reviewed their organizations' programs, could they honestly say that seeking to empower the poor is one of their top agenda items?

Is it not heresy to largely ignore the second most common theme in the Bible and then pretend that one is offering biblical Christianity to one's people? If Ezekiel 3 is right, will God not hold evangelical leaders accountable for their widespread failure to teach their people about God's concern for the poor? Evangelical leaders have four options:

1. The radical option: You can preach fiery sermons and get thrown out. I don't recommend it.

2. The conformist option: Basically, you can preach and teach what the people want to hear, throwing in an occasional word about the poor on World Hunger Sunday.

3. The calculating option: You resolve to lead your people into greater concern for the poor, so you calculate just how much they can take without getting really upset. You push them, but never to the point of endangering your job. At the end of the day, this is just a more sophisticated

version of the conformist option, just a careful assessment of what the market will bear.

4. The Spirit-filled, costly option: You decide you would rather have Jesus than parsonage or pulpit or presidency. You decide to lovingly, gently, clearly teach all that the Bible says about justice for the poor.

And what will such an option lead to? Embracing a biblical balance of prayer and action, preaching and modeling, evangelism and social ministry, worship and mission will often lead to transformed, growing congregations.

But not always. Sometimes they throw you out. But unless you are ready to risk that, it means that no matter how you rationalize it, no matter how you massage your conscience, you really worship job security more than Jesus.[1]

These words are pointed enough to make any Christian leader pause and examine the priorities of his or her work and influence. Being just as guilty as any in my past leadership experiences, and being at risk of making choices that conform to Western values, I acknowledge this call for change is first and foremost directed to those with the gift and responsibility for influence. When Western churches see and hear leaders communicate and demonstrate the vision of global, self-emptying, Christ-like compassion as lived out in the New Testament Church, we will be on the way to eradicating needless suffering. We will then recover our voice of credibility in a world that has dismissed Christianity as another outdated institutional world religion for the less educated or unenlightened. We will see unified, Christ-following communities engaged in lightening burdens of need and contributing to community development in the most desperately poor corners of the world. However, the first people to make this very personal commitment to change have to be those who are looked toward to demonstrate the way forward: its leaders.

Hard Core Heart Questions for Leaders

This is not primarily a book about leadership. An exhaustive look at the issues of leadership and change in the context of the Church and the world would consume volumes. Many have written more than enough on these topics. However, since it must be leaders who first boldly live lives of self-emptying sacrifice and compassion, it is worth pausing to give leaders an opportunity to examine their motives, values, and priorities. Leaders have the ability to influence people solidly toward a life of compassion and selflessness, or they have the ability to lead people solidly in line with conventional cultural priorities. The latter takes no effort at all, but the former takes constant examination and renovation of the heart. The heart condition and character of leaders will directly affect their organizations. No matter how well we can present our motives as completely pure, no one has a 100% selfless objective; therefore, we must recognize the need instead to forcibly asking ourselves questions that constantly bring about self-awareness, teachability, and humility. Leaders may know how to conceal selfish motives with a spiritual-looking presentation, which makes it all the more important that we constantly examine the true motives of our hearts. To leaders or those who could be, a few questions to consider:

- Am I more committed to my personal comfort, safety, and security than to the terrifyingly hopeful leaps of faith like we read about in Hebrews 11?

- For whose benefit, really, do I lead or serve?

- What is my first reaction when someone else is credited with my ideas or thoughts?

- Do I secretly feel my experience, title, or role entitles me to more than anyone else that I lead?

- Is my motive for an impressively large church building, a large staff, a large budget, large programs, and large attendance so that people will be impressed with me and my leadership?

- Do I look for opportunities for people to see me as a servant?

- Am I initially defensive when criticized, instead of vulnerably looking for the "nuggets" of fertilizer for my personal and professional growth? When someone is critical of me, regardless of their motives, do I defend myself by thinking of some reason to invalidate the critique?

- Do I attach my emotional well-being to praise, affirmation or agreement of others instead of the confident knowledge that I am doing what God called me to, regardless of the approval of man?

- How much of my need to be "up front" is driven by insecurities related to my sense of value?

- Do I look for opportunities to abdicate responsibility, or pass off things I don't like to do, and call it "empowerment" versus helping people to be used by God, even at the risk of losing the spotlight?

- Do I feel defensive when people do not agree with me or hold differing opinions about matters close to my heart?

- When someone close to me succeeds publicly, is my first reaction to feel minimized, threatened, or devalued?

- Do I secretly compare my work or actions to that of others?

- Do I "covet" the gifts and strengths of leaders who have more notoriety or resources than I?

- Am I tempted to exaggerate stories or facts to cause people to think better of me or to be more impressive or persuasive?

- Is my quest for excellence and achieving results more about people thinking well of me than about serving God?

- Am I jealous when other leaders appear to have success I don't?

- Do I feel the need to control people or situations to bring about favorable outcomes, or am I content to do my best to influence and then leave the results to God?

- Am I trying to "fix" or change people for my benefit or comfort versus God's glory and purposes?

- Lastly…am I willing to ask three of the people closest to me to answer these questions honestly on my behalf?

If you are like me, a few quiet moments with these questions on a regular basis will continually wring self out from your heart and leadership. Honest answers will produce a spirit of repentance that creates the environment of humility necessary for truly powerful and effective leadership.

The genesis of a transformed world is a transformed Church and the genesis of a transformed Church is transformed leadership. There are no shortcuts and no other options if a global movement of compassion and justice is to be more attractive than the perpetuation of the status quo of Western Christianity. Leaders and followers alike must get to the point where we are more troubled by the reality of the status quo than the discomfort of change. We must be more scared by a Church and world that doesn't change than fearful of what this change will mean for our personal and corporate lives.

Chapter 10 - So now what?

1. Give some practical examples of where you have seen leaders either positively or negatively influence people in regards to generosity and the poor.

2. Identify some of the costs, specifically for leaders, if they are going to influence a group of people toward greater life-changing compassion.

3. What was your reaction and thoughts about Ron Sider's article about Christian leaders?

4. As a leader, would you be willing to ask someone close to you to fill out the heart motivation questions for you?

5. What is the role that servanthood must play for leaders who desire to impact the world through those they lead?

Chapter 11

The Scary Transformational Power of Total Dependence

A God of Comfort and Safety?

In all honesty, I have two very compelling but competing passions in my life: one placed there by the culture of this age and one by the Age to come. These drives are both attractive and yet mutually exclusive. The old self is drawn to comfort, safety, ease, and predictability. The new self is drawn to risk, miracles, spiritual adventure, and a pioneering creation of a new world. The old self is compelled to laze on the sofa of all the comforts this world has to offer. The new self is compelled to storm the gates of Hell for all that the next World has to offer. Do you see my problem? I so badly want to see God show up in the daily rhythms of life, but I also tend to expend energy *avoiding* the conditions needed for His presence!

Within the first couple of years of being a young pastor, I was asked to go and visit old Mr. Harold Carter. Harold was one of the founding members of the church and was an usher for more than 50 years. Every Sunday morning, he was at the church before everyone else, turning on lights, opening doors, and making sure there was a glass of water on the pulpit for whoever was preaching that Sunday. By the time I ended up on staff, Harold's health was failing and for a couple of years he was in and out of hospital. I didn't really know him that well when I was given the visitation assignment. All I knew was that I needed to go and visit Mr. Carter, to encourage him and pray for him. I expected the stereotypical conversation with a senior who would talk about his failing health and how young people today were falling off the spiritual wagon. I was expecting to listen, nod, smile, and pray. But Harold greeted me when I drove up to his small house and we never got off his driveway.

I remember asking about his house and how he came to live where he did. My idea of small talk turned into a conversation (more like a testimony) I will never forget. He told me that, as a young child, he and his father got on a boat in Vancouver, gave the steward five dollars, and asked to be taken as far upriver as five dollars would take them. After traveling about 60 miles up the Fraser River, Harold and his dad got off the boat and settled into a two storey farmhouse in the Fraser Valley. He went on to tell me story after story about how God looked after his family for many years. They had nothing and had to rely on God's provision.

One story that will remain with me forever was about how God demonstrated His power during the great flood of 1948. The whole valley was flooded by the Fraser River and thousands were left homeless from this disaster. Harold and his family were forced into the second story of their home because water filled the first floor about halfway up the wall. They were stuck. They knew they had to remain in the upstairs bedroom until the waters receded. After some time with no food, and no way to get food, the family was hungry and needed God's help. So Harold's father led the family in prayer, asking God to provide for their needs and help them in this desperate situation. Sometime shortly after praying this prayer, Harold told me he looked down from the second story bedroom loft and watched a salmon swim in through the front door and right into the pot belly stove. They were desperate and God provided in a miraculous way. Harold told me he would never again question God's faithfulness and ability to provide.

I was jealous: Harold had a relationship with God I longed for. But Harold had also experienced situations I would really rather avoid. My desire to not be in a situation where my family is hungry, or some other equally uncomfortable reality, competes against my desire to unquestionably see the hand of God in our generation. Along with our culture's sense of entitlement to comfort and safety, we expect that God, being all powerful, wants us to be comfortable and safe. To be clear, God promised to be our comfort, not to make us comfortable; He promised to be a place of safety, not to make us safe. God promised to be a strong tower, not make us perennially secure. God Himself, and the activities of His kingdom, are anything but comfortable and safe.

Effectively Erasing the Need for God

One of Western society's sacred cows is independence. And sadly, it is has also been seen by God's people as a core value. We strive with incredible resolve to be self-sufficient, protected from harm or discomfort. We create buffer zones of protection around ourselves and those we love. Damaging to a pride that has been conditioned by self-interest, it is embarrassing, and in many cases "unspiritual", to be discovered in a state of need, want, or weakness.

Borne of an understandable care for the future, those who lived through the pain of the Great Depression instilled in their children and grandchildren values of hard work, saving, conserving, protecting, and building nest eggs for the proverbial "rainy day," not to mention backup plans and personalized insurance policies. New ministry initiatives must come with proposals almost guaranteed for "success" before they are ever funded. While it is biblical to be wise in our consideration of these factors, like the ant who stores up food for the winter, we have *unbiblically* resolved to do all we can to erase risk or potential for harm or failure. In doing so, we have denied our need for God and consequently erased the wonder and excitement of seeing His active power and presence in and through the lives of His people. In our well-positioned independence, we have replaced God and His work. We have forgotten about and ignored Him, not necessarily on purpose, but simply because we think we don't need Him. In response, God has moved into the background of our lives, politely allowing us to live with the fruit of our independence.

I love watching small children with their parents. They cling to their moms and dads as if life itself is totally dependent on the constant confirmation of their closeness. The fact that they are completely reliant on their parents for absolutely everything produces an intimacy that rivals no relationship on this earth. When children hurt themselves, feel threatened, have need for food, or simply need to know they're loved, they beeline for their nearest parent and hang on for dear life. It is a precious gift from God to watch the way of loving parents with their most vulnerable children. Yet, something interesting happens as children get older. As they grow and develop, they gain independence and, as they figure out how to eat, go to the bathroom, find their way around, and gain a sense of personal security and safety, they begin to wander from their parents' side and explore their new found self-sufficiency. While this autonomy doesn't necessarily lessen the love of a parent for their child or a child for their parent, it does naturally result in a certain separation and distance. At this point, a specific effort needs to be made to continue the closeness of the relationship. In unhealthy situations, independence can eventually erode the relationship and continue distance.

The application is obvious. As our immediate and obvious need for God becomes less, so does the level of our intimacy and closeness. This centuries-old reality is commonplace for Him. Throughout all of Scripture we see the same pattern repeated over and over. God's people are in a situation of incredible risk and vulnerability and, because of that, they walk in an incredible closeness to Him. Their relationship is seemingly unbreakable and, as a result of this intimacy, God blesses His people out of the goodness of a Father's heart. He blesses them with material comforts and social security and what happens? They begin to forget about Him. They don't realize the need for Him anymore, and the beginning of a convenient distance sets in. That disconnection eventually results in secularization and conforming to the patterns of this world. The relationship is broken and people live in the consequences of their sin and separation. God, through prophets and preachers, tries to regain His people's attention and affection, but we don't even hear the warning, because we now care more about what God has blessed us with than we do about Him.

Eventually, God either lets His people live out the darkness of our sin, or He takes away all He has given us, the "idols" that caused self-reliance. Sooner or later, the pain of our sin and wickedness leaves us in a position of dependence and need for His deliverance. Motivated by the uninhibited love of a heartsick father for the prodigal, God runs to His children, bringing us home with great rejoicing. The intimacy and relationship has been restored, and the closeness God intended to have with His people has returned, at least until we are again blinded by His blessings. When we are, the whole episode repeats itself.

The story of God's interaction with His people throughout history tells the same, repetitive, non-fictional story. He blesses us out of intimacy, and because He blesses us we stop realizing our need for Him and forget about Him, and we live with the sinful results of our independence; then we again need His forgiveness and intervention, thereby producing the intimacy of reliance again. God's relentless, benevolent, and loving nature compels Him to bless His children, and our self-focused nature compels us toward independence when He does. When we continue in our self-sufficiency and independence, God enables us to put ourselves in positions of dependence or He eventually forces us into a situation of dependence. He loves us enough to put us into situations where all we have is Him. He loves intimacy with us enough to care more about our closeness than our comfort.

The Power of God or Else

One of my favorite Old Testament stories is the showdown on Mt. Carmel between Elijah and the prophets of Baal in 1 Kings 18. It's an amazing narrative of God's power and passion to capture His people's attention away from false gods. It also contains some great humor as Elijah makes the point that God is real. Israel was in one of those typical situations of forgetting about God and absorbing the religious practices of those around them, specifically when it was convenient. The Scripture points out that Israel's king at the time, Ahab, was more evil than any king before him. Ahab had married Jezebel, who was not from Israel, and he allowed her to bring her god Baal into the religious life of God's people. Jezebel was using her marriage to the king to try and wipe out God's prophets in order to give Baal the number one god spot. Ahab went as far as to build a temple for worshiping Baal and, the writer says, "[Ahab] *did more to provoke the anger of the Lord than any of the other kings of Israel before him*" (1 Kings 16:33).

At this point, it appeared that no one really cared except Elijah, the prophet of God. He spoke for God, declaring that Israel's punishment would be no rain during the next few years. The nature of this specific punishment was significant: Baal was the Canaanite god of the storm and, as such, should be able to control the weather. As punishment, God was making the point that He really was God, the only one in charge of the weather.

He was rendering Baal powerless and, through that, making a commanding statement of His power.

After three years of drought and famine, God sends Elijah to confront Ahab about his idolatry and lukewarm spirituality. When Elijah appears before Ahab, the tension and conflict is high: Ahab blames Elijah for Israel's suffering and Elijah turns the judgment around on Ahab's two-faced spirituality. To clear up the matter, Elijah challenges Ahab to an epic contest between the historical God of Israel and Baal, the god of the king's wife. He puts himself in a position of total dependence: if God doesn't show up, he'll be finished and God's name will be mud.

In front of the entire nation of Israel, Elijah sets up a contest to see which god is the real God, and tells everyone to follow the One who shows up. The prophets of Baal are to prepare an altar, put wood on the top, sacrifice a bull, and lay it on top of the wood. Elijah will do the same. The prophets of Baal will call out to their god to send down fire from Heaven to burn the sacrifice. The prophet will do the same. Whichever altar miraculously lights on fire will indicate the one true God and everyone should follow Him. So, the prophets of Baal set about their work, doing exactly as Elijah said, and call out to Baal to send fire from Heaven.

The prophets call out to their god from morning till noon and nothing happens. This is the funny part. Around lunch time Elijah comes to sarcastically mock the followers of Baal, *"You'll have to shout louder, for surely he is god? Perhaps he is daydreaming, or is relieving himself. Or maybe he is away on a trip, or is asleep and needs to be woken up*" (1 Kings 18). The prophets do as Elijah suggests and pray louder, trying to get Baal's attention. They go so far as to cut themselves with knives and swords all afternoon in extreme self-denial and devotion. But still, nothing happens to their altar.

Then, in front of all the people, Elijah builds an altar to specifically remind the nation of God's care and faithfulness in the past. He sacrifices the bull and puts it on top, just like the prophets of Baal. Then he deviates from the plan a little: Elijah digs a trench around the altar and asks for four large jugs of water to be poured all over the sacrifice, the wood, and the altar. Then, he has them douse it a second time, and then a third. The altar and the sacrifice are soaked, and water fills the trench around the base. Now, if I was putting my life and God's reputation on the line, trusting that my altar and sacrifice would miraculously light on fire, the last thing I would do is drench it with water three times! Why would he do this? Elijah puts himself in the terrifying place of faith where, if God doesn't show up, he's finished; but, if God does show up, it would unmistakably be Him. Elijah has created an even bigger perception of a massive gap between the smallness of our ability and the hugeness of the need. The prophet wants it to be clear to the entire nation and the prophets of Baal that there is nothing he could do to meet the need for fire. Then Elijah simply walks up to the soaking wet altar and asks

God to prove today that He is indeed God. The next verse says, *"Immediately the fire of the Lord flashed down from heaven, burned up the young bull, the wood, the stones and the dust. It even licked up the water in the trench. And when all of the people saw it, they fell face down on the ground and cried out, 'The Lord – he is God! Yes, the Lord is God!'"* (1 Kings 18:38-39).

Oh, how we need God to prove today that He is indeed God! However, we can't miss the gut wrenching and terrifying reality that Elijah created an environment of total and unmistakable dependence, creating the opportunity for God to display His power and presence. Today, we ask God to demonstrate His power without putting ourselves in a place of dependence for Him to do so. North American Christians hate being dependent or putting ourselves in situations where, if God doesn't show up, we are in serious trouble. However, no great demonstration of God's power and presence among His people is displayed without His servants putting themselves in scary places of absolute trust and dependence.

Hebrews 11 convincingly communicates that nothing of greatness happens apart from the manifestation of God's power, a power that requires people be firmly planted in circumstances of weakness and terrifying dependence. Noah took years to build a huge boat in the middle of the desert and, when he did, God showed up and it rained. Abraham packed up his family and moved and, only *after* he did, God showed him where he was going. Although far too old, Sarah had been promised that she was going to have a child and, when she was convinced, God provided Isaac. With complete confidence that God would provide, Abraham lifted the knife to sacrifice the child God provided and, *after* the knife had been lifted, God supplied an animal for the sacrifice. In complete weakness and trembling, Moses walked right into Egypt and told the most powerful man in the world to let God's people go; but it was only *after* he obeyed in total faith that God displayed His power over and over until Pharaoh relented. Only *after* Moses stepped into the Red Sea, with no option of going back, did God part the water so they could walk on dry land. Only *after* God's people marched around Jericho for seven days, in the most ridiculous display of military strategy, did God bring down the walls and hand over the land He had promised.

We are desperately due for the manifest presence of God. We are urgently in need for God to again display His power and presence in our generation. But it will not happen through a commercialized, professional Christianity. The wonders of God that draw people to surrender will not come because of our programs or strategically designed long-term plans. There is far too much risk of us taking the credit. God will wait to fall upon His people until we realize we are utterly incapable of accomplishing anything of eternal worth on our own and offer ourselves up in complete dependence. I'm not talking about putting ourselves in places of mild discomfort. I'm convinced that until we boldly risk everything to walk the fine line between faith and stupidity, God will continue in silence and allow us to be consumed with ideas of our own importance and significance as we strive to advance the Kingdom.

The Day the Mountain Moved

Until a few years ago, I used to lament thinking that these types of displays of God's power were reserved only for those who walked around in the times recorded in Scripture. However, as I have constantly prayed and asked God to renew His works in our day, I was amazed to hear a story of biblical proportions when God displayed His glory in Cairo, Egypt around 975 AD. While in Egypt, I was taken to visit what is known as the "Cave Church" built into the side of Mt. Mokattam. We were shown a massive Coptic worship center that had been carved out of the side of a mountain which was used as a quarry for the building of the ancient pyramids. On the platform, our tour guide showed us relics and the remains of someone called Simon the Tanner. I asked about the significance of Simon the Tanner and the history behind why this church was in such a place.

We were told that about 1000 years ago, Egypt was ruled by a Muslim Governor who enjoyed the entertainment of religious debates between leaders of different faiths. During one of these debates, the Governor found a way to prove that Christianity was false and that Islam was indeed the true faith. He confronted the Christian Coptic Pope with the passage from Matthew that says, *"Jesus told them, "I tell you the truth, if you have faith and don't doubt, you can do things like this and much more. You can even say to this mountain, 'May you be lifted up and thrown into the sea,' and it will happen. You can pray for anything, and if you have faith, you will receive it""* (Matthew 21:21). The Governor saw this as either an opportunity to move a massive mountain that happened to block his view, or to finally prove Christianity was false. The Pope was given three days to move the mountain or Christians must choose one of three options: turn to Islam, flee Egypt, or die by the sword. The Christians were in a situation where, if God didn't come through, they were dead.

So the Coptic Pope gathered all of the religious leaders and called on them to pray for an answer. This was a solution that couldn't be manufactured by man; they were desperately dependent on God. While praying, the Pope heard God tell him to go outside and meet a one-eyed tanner – a leather craftsman – named Simon, and that man would have the answer to how to move this mountain. Sure enough, the Pope walked out of his church and saw a one-eyed tanner walking down the street. The Pope pulled Simon into the church and told him what God had said and asked whether or not he knew what the Christians were supposed to do. Simon explained he had indeed heard from God and the Pope was to gather all of the Christians, the Governor and all of his followers and assemble at the base of the mountain. When everyone was gathered, the Christians were to fall to the ground and worship God saying, "...have mercy on us." They were to repeat this three times and, on the last time, they were all to rise and lift up the cross. As they did this they would see "the glory of God."

The Christian leader did exactly what Simon had instructed. He gathered everyone together at the mountain, and those from the two religions faced each other. The Christians poured out their hearts in fervent worship and prayer, and as they stood lifting up the cross there was a mighty earth quake and the mountain lifted high enough so you could see the sun shine underneath it. Every time they fell down to worship and stood up again, the mountain lifted. All of the Muslims fell down in fear, and worshiped God. The Governor pleaded with the Pope to stop because they were terrified. One account claims that the Governor proclaimed, "God is great; may His name be blessed. You have proven that your faith is a true one."[1] The Christians were given new freedoms and even protection from the Governor. God's power was displayed through the worship and complete dependence of His servants.

Hearing this story, my heart pounded with the anticipation that God would work like that in our day and it also pounded with fear wondering what kind of terrifying faith would be required of me to set the stage for God. If we want to see God do amazing things in our generation, we have to abandon our addiction to comfort, safety, and security, and either choose to put ourselves and our churches in situations of total dependence or wait for God to humble us into dependence. Neither will be comfortable, but the latter will be brutally painful. We envision a world that is transformed by God's power and presence. But for God to show up in His power and presence we need to give Him room to work and we must step back so He can be revealed. We need to take huge leaps of faith. We need to walk that fine line, having confident, blind faith and being willing to look completely foolish to those around us.

Why could we not think about taking large leaps of faith like the world changers we read about in Scripture? Why could we not sell everything we have and go to places of massive need? Why could we not choose to give away far more than we think we can afford? Why could we not commit to serving in a way that will cause us to run to God for help because we are so aware of our own inadequacy and weakness?

A Little Boy's Lunch

The mammoth challenges and brokenness evidenced by our neighbors nearby and those far around our world dwarf any thought that we can affect change despite any effort we can muster. When we are confronted with the depth of such need in the face of the apparent limitations of our personal resources, we are paralyzed by the conclusion that we can't do anything that will make a difference. Every time I travel to a developing country I battle the discouraging thought that whatever project we are working on is like walking up to an empty swimming pool with a thimble of water hoping to begin to fill the need. How can an average Westerner address the fact that 6 million children die every year from starvation? What can I do about the fact that there are about 12 million AIDS orphans in sub-Saharan Africa? No one needs to be convinced that so many are desperately poor. But very few know what to do about it apart from sending a few dollars to a favorite charity when they are particularly moved by the need.

Also, our conventional Western model of church has left people with the general idea that it is up to the "professionals" to do the work and the rest of us to observe and passively support from the sidelines. The common church attendee doesn't typically think their resources or skills can be of significant use in addressing people's deepest needs, never mind meeting global challenges of injustice and poverty. We have created and fostered a culture of religious and social passivity. This attitude, combined with the overwhelmingly enormous sea of need, paralyzes us into a catatonic and defeatist lethargy.

Shortly after my wife and I were broken by the immoral injustice of how many children needlessly died every day, we had the vision to start an organization that would engage churches from all over the Western world to do something about it. We were anchored to the hope that if the Church truly lived like Christ, we could one day see a time where children - like ours - could have enough food to eat, clean water to drink, and the opportunity for a future. The problem was we had nothing with which to start. We would need thousands of people, billions of dollars, a transformation in the priorities and purpose of the Church, and significant cooperation between large and small organizations around the world. However, all we had were a few volunteers, an unfinished basement to work out of, a small donation of office supplies, and an old computer.

Right around this time, friends of ours came to us with a message from John chapter 6. I'm sure I had read John 6 dozens of times and heard it a dozen more in Sunday School. Likely, even the most biblically illiterate knows the story of the day Jesus fed the 5,000. This was one of those times, however, that a passage of Scripture jumped off the black and white pages and into my life. For those with huge dreams and miniscule resources, this narrative is one to hold tightly to. At this point early in His ministry, Jesus was gaining a large following. After only a few of the recorded signs and miracles, John recounts how a large crowed had followed Jesus up on a hillside where He had gone to rest. It was around dinnertime and, knowing what was about to happen, Jesus turned to Philip and asked a rhetorical question, *"Where can we buy bread to feed all of these people?"* (John 6:5). I love the fact that, in this question, Jesus was subtly pointing out the disciples' complete inability to meet the need that was staring them in the face. Jesus' question would have led His closest followers to be overwhelmed by the inadequacy of their resources next to the immensity of the need. The first order of business in great manifestations of God's power is confirming mankind's utter hopelessness to accomplish anything of substance in our own power. Again, God is drawn to situations where there will be no mistaking Who's responsible for the great stuff that happens.

I would have loved to have seen the non-verbal dynamics to this situation. I can imagine a confused look on the faces of the disciples and the half-grin on Jesus' face. He drops this bomb of an expectation that this massive crowd should be fed because, would you look at the time, it's dinnertime. This food distribution obviously wasn't part of the daily schedule, and certainly wasn't discussed ahead of time. I can imagine that there was a long pause as the pressure mounts on Philip, whom Jesus asked for a solution. I wonder if Philip looked around at the other disciples to see if he had missed something earlier. Finally Philip had to answer Jesus, "Even if we worked for months, we wouldn't have enough money to feed them." There was no big box grocery store up on the hillside and, even if there was, it would take far more money than the group could earn from months of work. There was a massive need before the followers of Jesus and seemingly a complete lack of adequate resources to meet the need.

Dave Blundell

My favorite part of this story is what Andrew says next. Picture somewhere between 10,000-15,000 people sprawled over a hillside and all of a sudden, Jesus expects your leadership team to feed them all. Someone points out that this was obviously impossible given your limited resources. Trying to find a solution to this problem, Andrew pipes up and says, "Hey, look over there. There is a little boy who brought a lunch with him. He's got five loaves and two fish. (Pause) But hold on. What good is that going to do with this huge crowd?"

For even a brief moment, Andrew starts to look for a solution in this little boy's lunch. He had enough of a faith-filled thought to suggest something ridiculously miniscule compared to the size of the need. I want you to picture the little boy's lunch. These were not five loaves as we understand them. These were basically five dinner rolls. These were not two large salmon pulled out of the river. These were most probably the equivalent of two dried up sardines. Reading between the lines, I'm sure that before the words were even finished coming out of Andrew's mouth, he realized how ridiculous his suggestion sounded to the rest of the group. Oftentimes people of vision see the possible before the rest are able to. Visionaries are frequently thought of as idealistic dreamers who need to "get a grip on reality," and be more like everyone else. I'm sure even Andrew was convinced he had crossed the line between faith and foolishness to think that this measly offering could possibly ever be of any use in their dilemma.

240

After the disciples were thoroughly convinced there was no solution within their own resource pool, Jesus instructs them to have the crowd seated. He takes the five dinner rolls, thanks God, and distributes them among the crowd. He does the same with the two dried up sardines. And, between the time when the little boy hands over all he has and the moment the food starts to be distributed, a miracle happens. Jesus fills the gap between their need and the resources. I also love the fact that John thinks it's important to note that: (1) everyone ate as much as they wanted, and (2) there were enough leftovers to fill twelve baskets. Jesus didn't provide enough to give everyone a snack or stave off the hunger until they all went home. He extravagantly showed the full extent of His resources by overdoing the feeding program.

Likely there were thousands who never saw where this food came from. Likely many of them only knew that a basket of food came by and they ate. Definitely, we can assume the disciples learned a valuable lesson that day and discovered deeper things about this man who had turned their world upside down. However, we never hear anything more about the little boy who gave up his lunch to feed the thousands. At some point, a little boy whose mom had packed him a lunch surrendered what he had so that others might be able to eat. I'm sure that the person who was the most moved that day was this little boy. Using some more literary license, if I could put myself in this little boy's shoes that night as he was going to bed, I would be overwhelmed that

Jesus could have taken the very little that I had and used it to meet a world of need. This little boy would likely never doubt the difference he could make in this world. He would probably never minimize what he had to offer. He would remember the day that Jesus took the smallest possible resource to meet the largest possible need.

The parallel is obvious. Considering the injustice of global resource distribution in the context of the biblical picture of a compassionate Church, there is not one person who cannot offer as much as this boy. Jesus wants to take the small things and weak people of this world in order to demonstrate His power. This story neutralizes the excuse that we can't do anything about the needs of the world's poor. At the same time, it empowers us with the hope that each one of us has something to contribute and bring to Jesus so that He can demonstrate His love to a world that desperately needs it.

Chapter 11 - So now what?

1. Why do we work so hard to avoid putting ourselves in positions of dependence?

2. Why is dependence seen as a position of weakness in our society?

3. What role has dependence or weakness played in key spiritual times in your life?

4. Why do you think that God chooses situations of desperation in which to demonstrate His power and presence?

5. In which areas of your life would it be the hardest for you to be dependent?

6. Identify two or three ways you could put yourself in a position of dependence on God. What could you do to step out in faith so you would have to rely on Him?

7. Identify situations you know of, or have heard of, when God demonstrated His power when people were desperate or in a position of dependence.

Chapter 12

A Captivating Vision of a Preferred Future

The Story of Status Quo

Imagine with me that you are the pastor of a church that decides it is time to relocate. Your current building is old and very used and the leadership is leaning toward buying land and building a new structure for the congregation to meet and worship. The predominant rationale is that outsiders will be attracted to a new building. Your realtor has made you aware of a piece of property that would be perfect for the larger structure, and it's in the right price range. You go with a few of the deacons to take a look at the proposed property and realize that, while the land is perfect for a new church building, you're not too excited by the neighborhood. Around the property are a few small, run-down, older homes. You now understand why this land is such a good deal. The obvious lower class demographic understandably brings down the value of this property. As you deliberate with the other leaders, the consensus is that the price is too good to pass up and besides, maybe you could reach out to your immediate mission field.

You buy the land and take a couple of years to raise the cash needed for the building. The architect's drawings are beautiful. While the building ends up being bigger than you and the other leaders had first envisioned, the congregation is excited about what they now see on paper and the leaders decide to stretch even further financially, buoyed up by overall enthusiasm of the people.

The time comes to break ground and start the construction. As you and the leadership team travel out to the site to make preparations for a groundbreaking ceremony, you notice that in the past couple of years the neighborhood is more impoverished and dilapidated than you had remembered. In fact, you see that a few more shacks have popped up. You quietly worry how the congregation will feel about the location as the project progresses. Maybe the location will be a bigger deal than you had first thought.

The day of the groundbreaking service arrives and many of the church members drive into the empty field of tall grass and weeds. The denominational leaders arrive to represent the Fellowship. You have arrived early to make small talk, and you notice the glances of some of the people toward their new neighbors as they walk from their cars to the plastic chairs that have been set up, and you wonder what they are thinking. A few of the neighborhood kids watch the gathering crowd from a distance. Your anxiety level rises as you compare how the church kids are dressed to the kids that have emerged from their run-down homes. Your inside voice has remained quiet until an affluent and influential family, and potential large donor, approaches. The father breaks the tension and says sarcastically, "Nice neighborhood! I sure hope that we get insurance for our new church if you're looking for my support." Your awkward laugh and following silence confirms your fears about what people are thinking. "Oh, we'll make sure we are adequately insured," you reply. At the end of the day, you discover that another mother with small children commented to your wife that she worries about the influence of the neighborhood children, because she has heard rumors about some of the families from this area.

The construction goes along well with its typical delays and setbacks, but overall the leadership is happy that things are relatively on schedule and on budget. As the exterior work is being completed and the interior finishing is starting, your excitement compels you to drive by the construction site every day as you go home from work. However, as the building more and more resembles the beauty of the architect's drawings, you are sobered by how much the new church building stands out in stark contrast to the growing population of unwanted neighbors.

Next to your impressive project, the homes and shacks more and more resemble an urban slum.

A couple more months pass and the project nears completion. The cleanup of the construction site is followed by the landscaping contract, presenting a manicured, postcard-looking picture. You are filled with excitement about the completion of the project but also with anxiety due to its location. Thankfully, the move-in goes well and everyone is enjoying their new spiritual home. Surprisingly, you are relieved that comments about the neighborhood have been almost non-existent, leading you to hope that maybe the congregation isn't as concerned about the surrounding influence as you are. However, remembering the conversation you had with a major donor, you double check to make sure you are adequately insured.

Several months of programs, services, potluck dinners, Christmas programs, and kids clubs go by. Church attendance really hasn't increased as you had hoped it would after having a new and welcoming facility. The couple of new families that have been attending only offset those who left because they were opposed to a new construction project. Yet, there still seems to be an air of excitement because of the new facility and you decide to remain upbeat, at least in public. You determine to make a renewed effort to encourage your friends to invite theirs.

You have been in the building now for almost a year and are there one Saturday afternoon setting up for the next day's service. There is a knock on the glass door in the lobby and you turn to see someone who you suspect is from the immediate community. You had wondered when the day would come that someone would come and ask for assistance, and this was the day. Recognizing the visitor as one of the older children who lives in the home behind the parking lot, you let him in and sit down on a pew in the lobby. The child timidly explains that his family has run out of food and was wondering if the church could help in any way. Fearful of what the family will do with cash and consistent with the church benevolence policy, you politely explain that you would come the next week to visit his home and see what you could do. "Thanks for coming by. Jesus loves you!" you assure him. As you watch the child walk away from the church, you feel a sense of pride about how you handled the situation and, besides, it was about time that you acted on the intent to get to know the mission field in your backyard. As you drive home thinking about the encounter, you are also affirmed in your decision, realizing that you have to be careful of the precedent you are setting. If you help one family and the others hear about it, you never know how many will come asking for money. And frankly, money is a little tighter than it once was with all of the expenses of the relocation. There are always those unanticipated expenses that come with a move.

Late one morning halfway through the next week, you remember what you said to the young man who came by on the weekend, and decide now is as good a time as any to go and meet the adults in the home. Walking through the parking lot toward the home you think is his, the poverty you knew existed in the backyard looks even worse than you had imagined. As you get closer, your senses begin to tell you that your neighbors live a very different life than you do, and you are fighting judgmental thoughts about their cleanliness and lack of work ethic. The previous worries about how the congregation would mix with the neighborhood creep back into your mind. As you approach the door of the home you realize that you are in fact in a different world than the one you live in. The door is barely holding onto the rotted 2x4 frame and it is held closed with a wire wrapped around a bent nail. The stench of sewage and human filth make you extremely hesitant to go further. The outside walls of this home are actually made of mud and twigs that, from much further away, just looked like brown stucco. The roof is corrugated tin, nailed to various pieces of old used wood that were being used as trusses and frame. You force yourself to knock on the door and a woman opens, peeking around the door but saying nothing. In that moment of initial silence, you see a few children sitting on a dirt floor and wonder why they aren't in school. You introduce yourself, telling her you are from the church across the parking lot, and the woman motions for you to enter by turning her head.

You can't even believe what you are seeing. The children are lethargic and wearing only tattered shirts, playing with household garbage that had been saved and fashioned into playthings. In one corner, there is a plank of old plywood sitting on the ground with a few plastic cups and bowls and a large soup spoon. You are given the only thing to sit on, a rusted bed frame, and the woman of the home sits on the floor on a mat beside the children. As you really take a good look at the woman for the first time, she seems too old to have children this young. She is too embarrassed to speak and you try to act comfortable in an incredibly uncomfortable situation. You speak first by explaining, "Your son came by the church on the weekend and asked for some assistance, and it is our church's policy not to give out money. Instead, we would like to visit and assess the needs of the family asking for help. So please, explain the situation you are in and why you are asking for help."

In a hushed voice and with a foreign accent the woman apologetically responds by saying, "I'm sorry that he came to the church; he did it without my knowledge or blessing. The other day his younger sister passed away from diseases and hunger. In fact, I am the grandmother to these children. Their father has been gone for quite some time now, and their mother passed away delivering her fifth baby, the baby who died last week. The boy who came to the church works in a field about two miles away earning about seven dollars a week and that is what we have to make do with. I am able to feed the children once every other day, but there is no money to pay their school fees or buy medicine. I am too sick to work, but I manage to grow some stalks of corn behind the house once or twice a year. That helps a bit. When it rains we have clean water, but during the summer season, we have to walk to a nearby cow field to take water from the pond. During the summer we are constantly sick. We would be grateful for anything the church could do for us. Thank you for visiting us today."

After sitting in silence for what seems like forever, the first person to move is the grandmother. She leans back toward the corner of the sitting room and lifts up an old plastic bag which has been covering half a dozen small, underdeveloped cobs of corn. She grabbed two of the larger ones and, while on her knees, offers them to you. Everything inside of you wants to reject her gift but you receive them thinking that not to would be worse. She repeats her appreciation, "Thank you for coming over from your church and visiting us this morning."

Realizing the visit is finished and your heart is transformed, you stand up, shake the hand of your neighbor, and turn toward the door. One of the older children unwinds the wire from the nail and opens the door for you. Saying thank you once more, you turn toward the church to go home. As you start the walk across the freshly paved parking lot, with your experience still overwhelming your attention, you look toward the new church building and stop your slow walk back.

The contrast between these two worlds makes you evaluate the entire process of the past few years. Every conversation about the "need" to relocate and build, every review of the architect's drawing, every thought about what the congregation would think about the new neighborhood is re-evaluated in this moment. Standing there looking at the church, you burn with anger remembering the donor's concern for adequate insurance to protect the building from "these people," and your face flushes red as you remember agreeing with him. You continue walking toward the church and, with a cob in each hand, you can't even bring yourself to go back inside such a place of worship so extravagant compared to the home you just visited. Instead, you walk toward your car, reaching in your pocket to unlock the doors. You get in and lay the gifts you were given on the seat beside you. Staring at them and sitting in silence, your eyes fill with tears as it sinks in that your spiritual poverty far exceeds the physical poverty of your new friends. This day changed everything.

A Contemporary Biblical Vision

How can our geographical distance from desperately poor and starving neighbors enable us to callously ignore the reality and the injustice of their poverty? This story is far from fictional. Although the situation of poverty in the story might seem unrealistic in a North American setting, my point is that there is absolutely no difference between the poor at the end of our parking lot and the poor at the end of a plane ride. The world has become exponentially smaller in the past couple of decades, and the Western Church is accountable to act with what we have and what we know.

Holding the biblical vision of a compassionate Church against the backdrop of completely unnecessary extreme suffering, we should be filled with anger and hope that things should and can be transformed. If we as leaders stop trying to simply modify Christian behavior, and instead facilitate encounters with the presence of God that conform our values to His, we will start to see pockets of change around the world; with the seeds of transformation planted, we'll see the translation into a movement of love and compassion that would witness the eradication of needless suffering. As I have said, the most significant factor that prevents this picture becoming reality is our spiritual poverty in the West. Throughout history, we have seen precious few examples of the biblical vision of justice and compassion lived out by God's people in a way that creates even a dent in addressing unnecessary and unjust suffering. The time has never been more perfect for a renewal of the Church and a resulting renovation of the world. There is nothing but obedience that prevents the Church from changing the world.

During this generation, we could see tens of thousands of churches from the Western world strategically connected to and engaged in immediate relief and long-term development with small communities around the developing world. And, as it should, the Church would take a front seat role in leading this dream of a world without needless suffering. If the vast majority of Western churches, no matter how small, partnered with the global development community and with local leaders in developing countries, not only would communities rise out of poverty, but the world would also take note of the Church for what she was intended to look like.

Thankfully, more and more leaders in our North American churches are beginning to desire greater input and impact in addressing some of the world's most pressing needs. God's people are rediscovering the essence of what it means to follow Christ and thereby restore the reputation of the Church in the world. A greater value and priority toward simplicity, compassion, and social justice is emerging, resulting in a generosity that serves and assists the world's billion poorest people.

Specifically studying and writing about the global engagement of local churches in the U.S., Princeton University sociologist and religious studies professor Robert Wuthnow recently published a book called *Boundless Faith: The Global Outreach of American Churches*. Based on excellent scholarly research, Wuthnow comprehensively describes the significant movement of local churches looking to engage directly in global issues. Citing factors of globalization, mass communication, technology, access to travel, a rising social conscience and entrepreneurial church leadership, he states, "U.S. congregations are increasingly trying to reach beyond their local communities and do so with whatever resources they can muster".[1] Consistent with my work, initially with churches in Canada, the trends and realities Wuthnow describes in American churches are extremely exciting indicators in the march toward a vision of a Church that would transform the world. Wuthnow writes:

> As the world becomes increasingly interdependent, Christianity in the United States is becoming transcultural, responding to the realities of globalization by actively and intentionally engaging in activities that span borders. Transcultural congregations give priority to programs that honor their commitments at home but also seek to be engaged in the lives of others around the world. A transcultural orientation connects local commitments with churches, communities, organizations and individuals in other countries. Church leaders increasingly stress having a vision that transcends the interests of those who gather for worship each week at the local church building. They contend that a congregation focusing only on itself becomes insular. They want their members to understand that the Christian gospel

is for all of humanity, and they encourage members to become informed about and engaged with the full range of conditions to which Christian teachings apply, whether this involves evangelization, feeding the hungry, ministering to the sick, serving as peacemakers, caring for children or showing hospitality to the stranger. [2]

This momentum created out of direct engagement by local churches in the lives of those who suffer is like a sunrise that informs the dark that the night is over. This new development of global Christianity presents an unprecedented opportunity for the Western Church to have historical impact. Furthermore, relationships that are built between churches and believers from developing countries will also breathe new spiritual life, radically alter our value systems, and reorder our personal and corporate priorities. Meeting and serving Christ in the lives of the poor will transform individual Western believers and quicken the desperately needed overhaul in the Western Church.

The hope and vision I have for a Church that could transform the world comes not only from theory or inspirational biblical references, but also from firsthand experience. Over the past few years, we have assisted Western churches to partner with churches and organizations in the developing world to provide clean water; build schools and increase access to basic education; provide food for the hungry and increase food security; assist with job creation and income generating activities; build homes;

care for orphans and widows; clothe the naked and cold; provide access to health care; treat basic but life-threatening illnesses; and send teams of volunteers to participate in appropriate relief and development activities. We have witnessed changed lives and the transformation of people, churches, and communities. What we have seen has confirmed a reason for hope.

On my most recent trip to an extremely poor, rural area of western Kenya, I was struck by how simple it can be to affect change in the lives of people. Within the period of a few short months, I saw Kenyan families move from the desperation of sickness and starvation to hope from growing enough food to feed their families and selling the surplus for medicine and school fees. This massive change was the result of the simple gift of seeds, a few garden tools, and little bit of training. I saw villages that had been suffering disease and death from drinking filthy water become healthy and strong. I was told that people are able to work and their children are able to go to school again because of a reduction in waterborne illnesses. This massive change was the result of simply getting access to the clean water that lies just metres under their homes. Children who had been orphaned by AIDS, abused and starving, walking alone from mud hut to mud hut hoping for the slim chance of the smallest scrap of food, became part of a family of orphans and attended school like the other children from the village. This massive change, in the life of one child, is the result of a $75 per month donation. It is often so easy to change or save someone's life.

We have all of the necessary ingredients for spiritual and social transformation. We have a historically well-resourced Western Church with an ever increasing focus on justice and compassion with a greater capacity to access the poorest areas of the globe. However, churches and grassroots community groups in the West often simply don't know where to begin to address the complex issues and systemic causes of extreme poverty. I have heard countless pastors and Christian leaders say, "We all know there is need and that we should be doing more, we just don't know where to start." If more NGOs and relief and development agencies could come alongside these small funding groups and assist them by providing guidance and expertise in the best practices of relief and development, we could remove the last major obstacle to a historic mobilization of the Church. Those of us from the para-church and NGO community must stop seeing local churches as a target for our programs and projects. We must stop trying to compete with each other for donors and donor groups, selling them on why we are the organization that is most worthy of their support. Instead, there is great hope and potential if we work with each other, assisting churches and other funding groups with the implementation of their projects, rather than trying to convince them to assist us with ours (see Appendix A).

If relief and development agencies could successfully partner with each other at a global level, and fully integrate with Western funding groups and developing country community development leaders and indigenous development solutions, we would see a world transformed. This vision necessitates a comprehensive shift in everything from how agencies are funded to how they go about the business of relief and development. The "business as usual" model sees a fragmented and continuously underfunded reality in which poverty and suffering expands faster than our ability to respond. We need to lay down our brands and our obsessions to be recognized as the only organizations worth supporting. There are millions of people and billions of dollars available to be mobilized and invested in global partnerships that could eradicate extreme poverty if only we could sacrifice our organizational arrogances on the cross of humility. Again, the cost of not changing is far greater than the cost of change.

We live in a day where historians will write one of two extremes about the Church. If we bow to status quo, historians will record a Church that wasted an opportunity to eliminate needless suffering because we cared more about our own excessive comfort, insulated safety, and perception of security than the most basic needs of half of the world's population. We will be known as religious professionals that turned following Christ into a commercialized veneer that protected us from any need to get our faith dirty or make it real. If nothing changes, I believe that historians will record this century as the most tragic in ecclesiastical history.

On the bright side, the history books have not been written yet, and there is still time to write a better version. Christian leaders need to be a prophetic chorus of voices that declare a single-mindedness about fostering a spiritual environment that results in a metamorphosis of core values and priorities. If, at the same time, we care more about transformation than job security, we will one day read about a Church that changed the world. Historians will write about a Church that became completely fed up with religious form and façade. History books will record how Western Christians en masse chose simplicity rather than contemporary materialism and consumerism. We will read about unprecedented generosity that was countercultural to a narcissistic and hedonistic society. Church history will state that Christians became true followers of Christ and mirrored His life of selfless purpose that transformed global social reality.

History will record one extreme or the other. There will be no middle ground because of the unjust and extreme imbalance between the "Christian" West and the developing world. The path of least resistance, the status quo, will result in a tragic condemnation. The much more difficult road to a global movement of generosity, though, will be worth every uncomfortable and faith-filled uphill step.

This biblically founded vision must be born in and lived out by the community of God's people. And it will only be lived out by the community of faith when we live it out first as individuals within this community. If I close my eyes and picture what the world so urgently needs, it is a Church that has a striking resemblance to Jesus. It is a Church that cares far more about getting its hands and feet dirty than upholding religious customs and institutions. It is a Church that has as its primary purpose intimacy with Jesus and is bursting with light that spills out into the darkest areas of the world. It sets the bar high for self-emptying love and leads the rest of the world in living out God's image that resides in all people. It is a Church that prioritizes the needs of others over its own wants, that sets a new standard of modesty and simplicity so that it can give away far more than it holds on to. It is a church that is respected by the global community as a major player and leader at the table of compassion and development. There are millions of people from the affluent West waking up to both the need and the ability and responsibility to do something about it. It has never been more vital or exciting to be part of Church renewal and its potential impact on the world.

So, where do we go from here? Recognizing that the root cause of social injustice is our spiritual poverty, the genesis of this personal and corporate vision for transformation is a personal and corporate repentance: a 180 degree turn from our current state.

In a spirit of self-examination and humility, read the following calls for repentance that are every bit as relevant today as they were when spoken so long ago.

From Revelation 3 to the Church in Sardis, calling for repentance for religious form without substance:

> I know all the things you do, and that you have a reputation for being alive—but you are dead. Wake up! Strengthen what little remains, for even what is left is almost dead. I find that your actions do not meet the requirements of my God. Go back to what you heard and believed at first; hold to it firmly. Repent and turn to me again. If you don't wake up, I will come to you suddenly, as unexpected as a thief. (Revelation 3:1-3)

From Revelation 3 to the Church in Laodicea, calling for repentance from spiritual apathy that stemmed from their wealth:

> I know all the things you do, that you are neither hot nor cold. I wish that you were one or the other! But since you are like lukewarm water, neither hot nor cold, I will spit you out of my mouth! You say, 'I am rich. I have everything I want. I don't need a thing!' And you don't realize that you are wretched and miserable and poor and blind and naked…I correct and discipline everyone I love. So be diligent and turn from your indifference. Look! I

stand at the door and knock. If you hear my voice and open the door, I will come in, and we will share a meal together as friends. Those who are victorious will sit with me on my throne, just as I was victorious and sat with my Father on his throne. (Revelation 3:15-17,19-21)

From Amos 5, calling for repentance from spiritual apathy that results in social injustice:

Listen, you people of Israel! Listen to this funeral song I am singing: "The virgin Israel has fallen, never to rise again! She lies abandoned on the ground, with no one to help her up…

"How you hate honest judges! How you despise people who tell the truth! You trample the poor, stealing their grain through taxes and unfair rent. Therefore, though you build beautiful stone houses, you will never live in them. Though you plant lush vineyards, you will never drink wine from them. For I know the vast number of your sins and the depth of your rebellions. You oppress good people by taking bribes and deprive the poor of justice in the courts. So those who are smart keep their mouths shut, for it is an evil time.

"Do what is good and run from evil so that you may live! Then the Lord God of Heaven's Armies will be your helper, just as you have claimed. Hate evil and love what is good; turn your courts into true halls of justice. Perhaps even yet the Lord God of Heaven's Armies will have mercy on the remnant of his people. Therefore, this is what the Lord, the Lord God of Heaven's Armies, says: "There will be crying in all the public squares and mourning in every street. Call for the farmers to weep with you, and summon professional mourners to wail. There will be wailing in every vineyard, for I will destroy them all," says the Lord...

"I hate all your show and pretense—the hypocrisy of your religious festivals and solemn assemblies. I will not accept your burnt offerings and grain offerings. I won't even notice all your choice peace offerings. Away with your noisy hymns of praise! I will not listen to the music of your harps. Instead, I want to see a mighty flood of justice, an endless river of righteous living." (Amos 5:1-24, emphasis added)

The very idea of repentance implies the action of going in the opposite direction. Once we have agreed with God that our spiritual poverty has led to social injustice, true repentance will only happen when we are living different lives with different consequences. Real contrition will result in a growing value on, and culture of, giving and compassion that lead to sustainable change.

It would be naïve of me to think that followers of Christ could once and for all escape the cycle and pattern of spiritual death and rebirth. No matter how "right" our generation gets it, any new awakening is likely to be followed by an eventual degeneration back into spiritual apostasy and ignorance of the poor. Throughout history, new movements of spiritual renewal and social justice sooner or later begin to slowly turn in on themselves. They drift away from the values and priorities they were originally founded on and morph into another religious institution. While I pray that won't be the case with our generation, I realize that precedent is not in our favor.

That said, I also realize that throughout church history God has a habit of doing new things through movements that emerge out of institutional religion. Out of healthy dissatisfaction and discontent with the status quo, new life springs from what looks like a spiritual wasteland. God, in His sovereignty, fulfills His purposes through the life cycle of new movements just as He renews the natural landscape after a forest fire. He allows His people to stray from intimacy and effectiveness to a place of spiritual desolation; and, eventually, a remnant of a passionate and purposed few emerge to seek Him for a new work for their generation. While I fully expect the same, I also do so with a hope and vision that at least our moment in church history will record one of the few epic times that God's people lived up to our purpose and altered the course of civilization.

Thinking and talking in these terms can very easily lead people to agree in principle and yet leave the job for someone else to do. This is one of those issues that lends itself to thinking it's always someone else's responsibility to act, it's someone else that must give more. The government must allocate more to international development. Philanthropists like Warren Buffet or Bill Gates should donate their billions. Or the leadership in developing countries must change its ways. But obviously, if everyone had that mentality, no one would do anything. While these ideas or hypothetical comments are true to a large degree, it is first up to us as individuals to bring the seemingly small choices we make into alignment with Christ's priorities. The daily decisions with regard to our time and treasure become the patterns that reinforce our priorities.

Before we finish our journey together as writer and reader, I, as one who is continually working through my own "so what?" to these issues, would fail if I didn't cause you to ask yourself, "How now shall I live?" In light of the unjust global imbalance of resources and the biblical picture of compassion, what must change in my soul and my actions that would reveal to the world that Jesus is alive and that He is completely broken by the suffering of the desperately poor? What must I do to bring my values and resulting actions into conformity to those of Jesus?

Again, the cost of remaining at the status quo is far greater than the cost of change.

Not long ago, someone asked me what my greatest fear was. I thought for a while about some of the things that scare me and then came to the same conclusion that motivates me to get up every day. Without a doubt, my greatest fear is to leave this world to my children the same way it was given to me. I can't bear the thought that I would have lived in a time when the Church could have handily dispensed the kind of justice and compassion that would have eradicated needless suffering, and yet have attempted nothing substantial toward that end. My greatest fear is to get to the end of my life and say regretfully, "I wish I would have done something."

Back to Your Story

After a few days of processing your trip to the other side of the parking lot and what your experience means for your church family, you call the leaders together. Your anger has turned to new resolve for new priorities and actions, at least for you. As the leadership team gathers at your request, not knowing the reason for the meeting, you feel isolated between two worlds and value systems. You are still all too familiar with the narcissistic and entitlement-based value system, dressed in religious form, that comprises the culture of your church. At the same time, you can't help but act on your own renovated value system that keeps your new neighbors solidly before your mind and firmly on your heart.

You start by telling the leadership of the events of a few days prior. You recount the entire experience, starting with your own feelings of spiritual pride that you were finally going past the parking lot, and ending with being completely undone by what you saw, heard, smelled, and felt. As you would expect, the spiritually and emotionally soft were visibly tuned in to your story and shaken by what you experienced. And as you would expect, there were a couple who were looking at you as if to say, "And what was the reason for this meeting?"

"We must change," you assert, "we can't keep on doing what we are doing. We can't keep going through the motions of religious activity, programs, and worship while we act as if the realities of what is happening in our backyard don't exist. Just a few meters away, people are dying from hunger and are suffering unimaginable poverty. Children are living and sitting in their own waste and growing up not able to go to school. All that's happening right beside us is completely avoidable, yet we communicate by our actions that our wants of extravagance are so much more important than their access to the basics of life. I can't believe I sent the boy away and proudly said, 'Jesus loves you!' when my actions said the exact opposite!"

Everyone is silent for a few uncomfortable moments and you feel you've done a convincing job setting the stage for the change you know is needed. The one leader who you were most concerned about and who was also most vocal was the first to speak after you. "You know the wealthy need Jesus too. If you have the gift or call to help those poor people, then you go ahead and do that. But as a church I feel we need to continue with our priorities and be good stewards and responsible with what God has given us in this new facility, inviting our friends to the church programs. We can take the benevolent offering once a month and give it to the Salvation Army. That's the kind of work that they do." You can see that this influential person has just moved those on the fence back to an acceptance of the norm.

The thought of status quo is more disturbing to you than the thought of what is required to risk change. Almost without thinking, you confidently declare, "I believe that we need to sell this building and our possessions, pool the money and assist that community at the end of the parking lot with the basics that are needed for life. There are plenty of other places to meet and to worship. We could share a building with another church. We could rent a community center. We have options, but they do not!" You are pointing in the general direction of the parking lot.

All eyes widen and a few protest the ridiculousness of your proposition with their body language. "Come on," says another leader, "don't you think that is a little extreme? We were all unanimous around this table feeling that God was directing us toward a move and toward construction. Are you saying that we were wrong or that God changed His mind about that?" Like watching a ping pong match, all of the eyes are back on you for a response. "What is extreme is the extreme suffering of those neighbors of ours! If it were our parents, who were looking after our children, we would go to any lengths and extremes to prevent the suffering of those we loved. But because we don't know them, we act as if it's okay to ignore their suffering. Week after week they watch us go about our spiritual motions and rituals, bringing in food for the banquets and potluck suppers while their children go to bed hungry most nights. As far as being convinced we *felt* God lead us to build this building, I don't have to wonder what God is saying about the poor. He managed to lace the entire counsel of Scripture with instructions and commands about looking after the poor, calling the ignorance of the poor as wicked as idolatry. It is pretty easy to say we have 'heard' the voice of God confusing His will with our desires. An extreme situation demands an extreme response. Choosing to sell our property and give what we have to the poor isn't reckless generosity, it is basic obedience!"

After several weeks of more informal and formal meetings, discussions, and Bible studies, the majority of the leaders have become passionate about the vision of compassion and the wonderful possibilities of change, both for those inside the church and for those on the other side of the parking lot. The most convincing motivation came when you took some of the willing leaders to go for that same walk through the parking lot. Introducing people from the congregation to your new friends produced the same soul-searching value shifts that left you undone by this injustice. It didn't take many visits before the vision of change became contagious for most of the church. People and groups within the church spontaneously met to plan how to become more generous and live simpler lives to enable greater giving. It didn't take very long before your leadership team was approached by another church in town who had heard about this new mission and passion. The other church in town was looking for a place to worship and suggested that they could pay for half of your new building and come up with an arrangement to share the resource of the facility. Holding services at different times and coordinating ministry schedules took a little work and adjustment at first, but it actually served to build unity among the two congregations. The two churches even decided to hold some special services and events together.

It was decided among your leadership team to use the funds from the other congregation to initially assist with food and clothing. A couple of the medical professionals in the church suggested that you could set up a free clinic on weekends twice a month. That was only the beginning. After discussing some options with the families from across the parking lot, funds were made available to assist the families to start small businesses and to enable their kids to go to colleges or trade schools. A few of the employers in the church were able to hire some of the men and older boys. Work teams would assemble on the weekends and assist widows with fixing their bathrooms and kitchens. Sunday mornings started to change. People from the community started to attend your services as well as the services from the other congregation you shared your building with. A discovery of compassion and generosity had an effect on giving. People were giving more, excited by the ability to see such great change with the shared resources from the church.

The movement toward compassion hasn't come without cost. Some of the most vocal opponents of the new priorities have left the church, taking some of their followers with them. More painful than the cost of the financial hit, some of those who left were close friends. As a leader, it seems as if some people will be your friend only when they agree with you. On the other hand, the pain of broken, apparently shallow relationships is less than the cost of not changing. By far, any loss is compensated by the results of a whole scale movement toward being a compassionate church. The spiritual temperature of the church has increased, evidenced by changed lives within the congregation as well as the neighborhood.

One evening a few months later, you sit down to read your Bible and you happen to be reading in the book of Acts. That night you read in chapter 4,

All the believers were united in heart and mind. And they felt that what they owned was not their own, so they shared everything they had. The apostles testified powerfully to the resurrection of the Lord Jesus, and God's great blessing was upon them all. There were no needy people among them, because those who owned land or houses would sell them and bring the money to the apostles to give to those in need. (Acts 4:32-35)

After reading this short description of the early church, you close your eyes and imagine what that would be like. But very quickly you realize that you don't have to imagine for very long. You are overwhelmed to tears by the wonderful discovery that your church now looks a lot like this one.

·

Chapter 12 - So now what?

1. What were your reactions to the fictional story in this chapter?

2. Does your spiritual community place a meaningful priority on showing a compassionate generosity that makes a difference in the lives of the poor?

3. Would you describe your or your church's involvement with the poor as a token obligatory afterthought, or as a defining core value evidenced in the use of resources? What observations contributed to your answer to this question?

4. How would your faith community (church, home group, youth group) need to change in order to prioritize ministry to the poor, locally and globally?

5. What would be the costs to make these changes?

Appendix A - Ok...So now what?
Introducing the "How"

There are enough great authors and great books out there that stir up great conversation about the brokenness of our world and what the Church should be doing about it. As I've stated, most Christian leaders don't need to be convinced about the suffering of people in developing countries or that the Church should be doing more about it. In our work with many churches, I have not once heard a leader say, "You know, I just don't think we want to do anything to help the poor."

I asked a number of church leaders, "If most churches want to help the poor, why aren't the poor being helped in such a way that it makes a maximum and sustainable difference?" One pastor put it this way: "You don't need to convince me that there is a lot of need in this world and that we as a church should be doing more to meet the need. What I need," he continued on, "is an organization that could help me with the how. I need an organization that can help us, as a church, with our project in a developing country." It was out of that expressed need that Hungry For Life (HFL) was formed. Essentially, what HFL does today is what I heard churches say they needed in order to have a strategic and sustainable impact in a small community in a developing country.

Instead of approaching churches and other funding groups to assist HFL with our projects, HFL assists these groups with their projects. HFL removes as many barriers and obstacles as possible for people in the West to be directly involved in international relief and development. Starting first with a comprehensive international focusing consultation, we serve by pairing a church or community group from the West with a small community or project in a developing country. We then continue to serve these groups in the design, implementation, and evaluation of their investments. The following diagrams illustrate the traditional model of how para-church or relief and development agencies interact with local churches or community groups in North America. This conventional model is then contrasted against HFL's approach and vision of engaging and involving those from developed nations in assisting those trapped in extreme poverty.

Traditional Para-Church Model

A church or group knows there is need in developing nations and they often raise funds to respond to the need but don't know how to invest resources in the most helpful way possible.

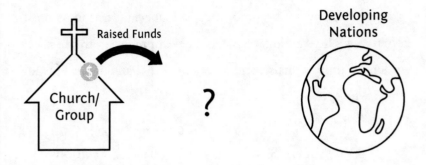

People and groups are then often approached by an international aid agency or a para-church organization that need to raise funds for their programs and projects. Most agencies use a portion of the funds raised for operational or administrative expenses and the remaining funds are then used for direct project related expenses.

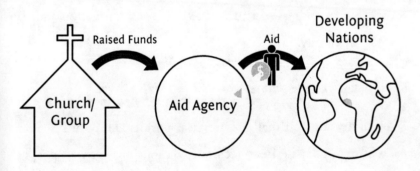

While there are many great organizations doing many great things, in the process of going and giving, often local churches, who have supported the projects and programs, feel uninvolved. This common model of international compassion and ministry doesn't usually impact people in Western nations who have a growing passion to become directly involved. Instead it most often leaves international relief and development up to the select group of "professionals", and misses the life changing benefits for those who give or go.

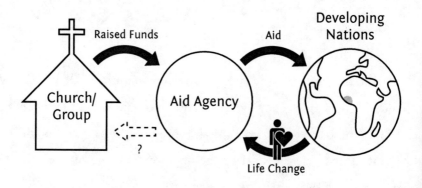

In an effort to be more effective in international compassion work and to address spiritual poverty in Western nations, HFL works differently.

Hungry For Life Model

Addressing spiritual and physical poverty, Hungry For Life was born out of a desire to facilitate relationships between people who have resources with those who need them. HFL exists to make it possible to take seriously the command to pay attention to the poor and oppressed in our world by helping remove the logistical obstacles for international relief and development work. HFL exists to serve the Church without taking out a portion of funds intended for international work. We believe there is a more effective model that will result in greater impact. Hungry For Life exists to come alongside churches and groups in North America to help them directly engage in projects of relief and development in developing nations worldwide.

We create international partnerships with national church leaders, missionaries, and Christian organizations in developing nations.

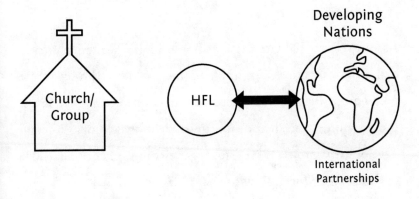

We also partner with churches and groups here in North America, to focus and involve them in long-term community development and relief projects by serving in the areas of project management and logistics.

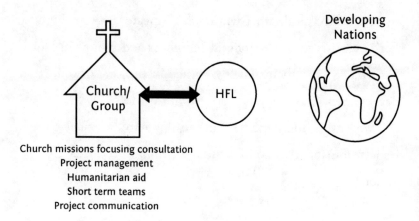

Church missions focusing consultation
Project management
Humanitarian aid
Short term teams
Project communication

We seek to facilitate relationships, bringing Western churches and groups together with international partners. Through these relationships, HFL serves those from developed nations to invest their resources and their people in international compassion and development projects. HFL makes the commitment that 100% of funds raised for projects are used for projects.

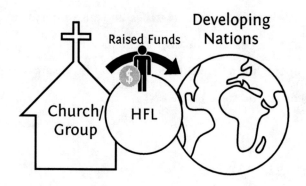

As churches/groups "spend themselves on behalf of the hungry," their lives are impacted and changed by the power and presence of Christ. That life change is brought back to the churches/groups, bringing passion and an increase in spiritual temperature.

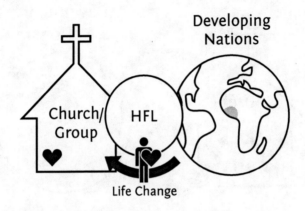

This life change then fuels greater passion, generosity, and involvement. Churches and groups send more of their people and resources and more lives are changed.

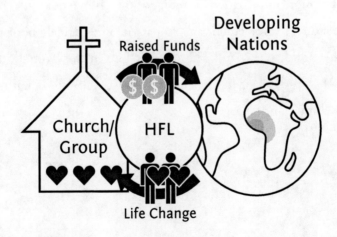

This further increases the passion and spiritual temperature of the Church in North America as well as further impacts the lives of the poor.

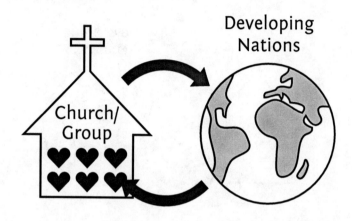

Our desire is that eventually we will be able to remove ourselves and the cycle of generosity and spiritual reciprocity will continue.

For more information about how your church or group could have a direct involvement and impact in a desperately poor part of the world, please call Hungry For Life in the United States at 801-979-6453 or in Canada at 604-703-0223 or email us at info@hungryforlife.org.

Appendix B – Recommended Websites

www.esa-online.org – Evangelicals for Social Action is an organization founded by Ron Sider to promote co-operation and Christian engagement in public policy issues related to poverty and injustice.

www.generousgiving.org – This is a website that serves to encourage generosity from a faith based perspective and communicate stories of how generosity is changing lives.

www.globalissues.org - This website looks into global issues that affect everyone and aims to show how most issues are inter-related. The issues discussed range from trade, poverty, and globalization, to human rights, geopolitics, the environment, and much more.

www.globalrichlist.com – This site is an eye opening online calculator that ranks your wealth compared to the rest of the world's inhabitants. It is a powerful tool to communicate the extreme imbalance that exists in our world.

www.hungryforlife.org – The website for Hungry For Life International, an organization seeking to address spiritual and physical hunger around the world.

www.kiva.org – Kiva is the world's first person-to-person micro-lending website, empowering individuals to lend directly to unique entrepreneurs around the globe.

www.poverty.com – A general site about the problems and causes of poverty and a list of solutions for those who want to act.

www.un.org/millenniumgoals - The Millennium Development Goals are global targets that world leaders set to unify developed nations around the issues of extreme suffering. The goals set out a number of key development issues and measurable results and targets for those who work toward eradicating needless suffering.

www.worldhunger.org – This website is a world hunger educational resource. The purpose of the site is to inform people about world hunger, facilitate communication with those working to address poverty, and promote solutions for hunger and poverty.

Appendix C – Recommended Reading

The following list of books represents what I would most recommend you read to delve deeper into the issues presented in this book.

1. *Rich Christians in an Age of Hunger: Moving From Affluence to Generosity* by Ron Sider

2. *The Life You Can Save: Acting Now to End World Poverty* by Peter Singer

3. *The End of Poverty: Economic Possibilities of Our Time* by Jeffrey Sachs

4. *Visioneering: God's Blueprint for Developing and Maintaining Vision* by Andy Stanley

5. *Holy Discontent: Fueling the Fire That Ignites Personal Vision* by Bill Hybels

6. *Revolution* by George Barna

7. *unChristian: What a New Generation Really Thinks about Christianity... and Why It Matters* by David Kinnaman

8. *Boundless Faith: The Global Outreach of American Churches* by Robert Wuthnow

References

2005 World Population Data Sheet. (2005). Retrieved 12 11, 2008, from POPULATION REFERENCE BUREAU: http://www.prb.org/pdf05/05WorldDataSheet_Eng.pdf

Aristides. (2009, 06 18). *In The Meantime*. Retrieved 06 18, 2009, from I Heart Revolution: http://i-heart.org/entry.php?intid=102

Barna, G. (2005). *Revolution: Warn Out on Church?* Carol Stream, Illinois: Tindale House Publishers, Inc.

Bartet, L. (n.d.). *Revival and Prayer*. Retrieved 04 11, 2009, from Revival: http://www.bayou.com/~lou2247/revpray.html

Berry Sr., D. P., & Reynolds, D. (n.d.). *Reflections On My Life: Louis Pasteur*. Retrieved September 12, 2008, from The Woodrow Wilson National Fellowship Foundation: http://www.woodrow.org/teachers/ci/1992/Pasteur.html

Bibby, R. (1986, May). Religion in the Twenty-First Century: The Canadian Case. Lethbridge, Alberta, Canada: The University of Lethbridge.

Blanchard, K., & Hodges, P. (2003). *The Servant Leader*. Nashville, Tennessee: Thomas Nelson, Inc.

Blomberg, C. L. (1999). *Neither Poverty Nor Riches*. Illinois: InterVarsity Press.

Blue Letter Bible. (n.d.). Retrieved 11 28, 2009, from Blue Letter Bible: http://www.blueletterbible.org/Bible.cfm?b=Jam&c=1&v=26&t=NLT#conc/27

Bourke, D. H. (2007). *The Skeptic's Guide to Global Poverty*. Colorado Springs, CO: Authentic.

Business Week. (2008). *Diet Industry*. Retrieved 12 13, 2008, from Business Week: http://bx.businessweek.com/diet-industry/news/

Cavey, B. (2005). *The End of Religion*. Oakville, ON: Agora Imprints.

Cellular News. (2006, 03 08). Retrieved 07 16, 2009, from Cellular News: http://www.cellular-news.com/story/16425.php

Chen, S., & Ravallion, M. (2008, 08). *The Developing World Is Poorer Than We Thought*. Retrieved 12 11, 2008, from World Bank: http://www-wds.worldbank.org/external/default/WDS-ContentServer/WDSP/IB/2008/08/26/000158349_20080826 113239/Rendered/PDF/WPS4703.pdf

Constantine I and Christianity. (2009, 02 14). Retrieved 02 18, 2009, from Wikipedia: http://en.wikipedia.org/w/index. php?title=Constantine_I_and_Christianity&oldid=270646719

Daft, R. L., & Lengel, R. H. (1998). Vision. In *Fusion Leadership: Unlocking the subtle forces that change people and organizations* (pp. 91-109). San Francisco: Berrett.

Edwards, J. (1743, 12 12). *Jonathan Edwards: On the Great Awakening.* Retrieved 04 10, 2009, from National Humanities Institute: http://www.nhinet.org/ccs/docs/awaken.htm

Effects of Revival. (n.d.). Retrieved 04 10, 2009, from The Welsh Revival: http://www.welshrevival.com/

Evangelical Fellowship of Canada. (2004). What are Canadians Saying to the Church. *Canada Watch, 9* (1), p. 6.

Food and Agriculture Organization of the United Nations. (2005, 11). *The State of Food Insecurity In The World.* Retrieved 12 11, 2008, from Food and Agriculture Organization: ftp://ftp. fao.org/docrep/fao/008/a0200e/a0199e.pdf

Gallagher, V. A. (2006). *The True Cost of Low Prices.* Maryknoll, New York: Orbis Books.

Gallup International. (2000). *Millennium Survey.* Retrieved 12 12, 2008, from Gallup International: http://www.gallup-international.com/

Global Issues. (2008). *Global Issues*. Retrieved 12 11, 2008, from Poverty Facts and Stats: http://www.globalissues.org/article/26/poverty-facts-and-stats#src22

Gordon-Conwell Theological Seminary. (2007). *Status of Global Mission 2008*. Retrieved 12 13, 2008, from Gordon-Conwell Theological Seminary: http://www.gordonconwell.edu/ockenga/globalchristianity/resources.php

Graves, D. E. (2000). *Amos*. Retrieved 02 19, 2009, from Atlantic Baptist University: http://www.abu.nb.ca/ecm/Amos00b.htm

History Of The Jesuits. (n.d.). Retrieved 04 10, 2009, from History World: http://www.historyworld.net/wrldhis/PlainTextHistories.asp?historyid=ab30

History of the Mendicant Friars. (n.d.). Retrieved 04 10, 2009, from History World: http://www.historyworld.net/wrldhis/PlainTextHistories.asp?HistoryID=aa90&ParagraphID=gfq#gfq

Hybels, B. (2007). *Holy Discontent*. Grand Rapids, Michigan: Zondervan.

Jacquet, C. (1991). *Yearbook of American and Canadian Churches*. New York: National Council of Churches.

Kinnaman, D. (2007). *unChristian*. Grand Rapids, Michigan: Baker Books.

Koszarycz, Y. (1999). *Constantinian Christianity*. Retrieved 02 18, 2009, from The ORB: On-line Reference Book for Medievil Studies: http://www.the-orb.net/textbooks/eccles/constantine.html

Maher, B. (2008, 09 29). Religulous. (H. Smith, Interviewer) CBS.

Malick, D. (n.d.). *An Introduction to the Book of Ezekiel*. Retrieved 02 19, 2009, from bible.org: http://www.bible.org/page.php?page_id=921

McLaren, B. D. (2006). *The Secret Message of Jesus: Uncovering The Truth That Could Change Everything*. Nashville: W Publishing Group.

McManus, E. R. (2001). *An Unstoppable Force*. Loveland, Colorado: Group Publishing.

Millennium Project. (2005). *Investing in Development: A Practical Plan to Achieve the Millennium Development Goals*. London, UK: United Nations Development Programme.

NASA. (2009, 05 07). *NASA Budget Information*. Retrieved 06 21, 2009, from National Aeronautics and Space Administration: http://www.nasa.gov/news/budget/index.html

National Defence. (2008). *Defence Budgets 1999-2007*. Retrieved 12 13, 2008, from National Defence and the Canadian Forces: http://www.forces.gc.ca/site/Reports/budget05/back05_e.asp

OECD. (2005, 11 04). Retrieved 12 12, 2008, from Organization for Economic Cooperation and Development: http://www.oecd.org/document/3/0,2340,en_2649_201185_34700611_1_1_1_1,00.html

Piper, J. (1997). *A Hunger For God.* Wheaton, Illinois: Crossway Books.

Ravallion, M., Chen, S., & Sangraula, P. (2008, 05). *Dollar A Day Revisited.* Retrieved 12 11, 2008, from World Bank: http://www-wds.worldbank.org/external/default/WDSContentServer/IW3P/IB/2008/09/02/000158349_20080902095754/Rendered/PDF/wps4620.pdf

Ronsvalle, J., & Ronsvalle, S. (2006). *The State of Church Giving through 2004* (16th ed. ed.). Champaign, Ill: Empty Tomb.

Ropelato, J. (2006). *Internet Pornography Statistics.* Retrieved 12 11, 2008, from Top Ten Reviews: http://internet-filter-review.topten-reviews.com/internet-pornography-statistics.html#anchor1

Rowell, J. (2006). *To Give or Not To Give?* Atlanta: Authentic Publishing.

Sachs, J. D. (2005). *The End Of Poverty.* New York: Penguin Books.

Scazzero, P. (2006). *Emotionally Healthy Spirituality.* Nashville: Thomas Nelson.

Sharma, S. R. (1998). *Leadership Wisdom from The Monk Who Sold His Ferrari: The 8 Rituals of Visionary Leaders*. Toronto: Harper Collins Publishers Ltd.

Sharp, T. (2008, February 20). *U.S. Defense Spending, 2001-2009*. Retrieved 12 13, 2008, from The Center for Arms Control and Non-Proliferation: http://www.armscontrolcenter.org/policy/securityspending/articles/defense_spending_since_2001/index.html

Sider, R. (2001, May). Are Evangelical Leaders On Their Way To Hell? *BC Christian News , 21 #5*.

Sider, R. J. (1997). *Rich Christians in an Age of Hunger* (5th ed.). United States of America: W Publishing Group.

Sider, R. J. (2005). *The Scandal of the Evangelical Conscience*. Grand Rapids, Michigan: Baker Books.

Siman, A. (2003). *How Much is Enough?* Grand Rapids, Michigan: Baker Books.

Singer, P. (2009). *The Life You Can Save*. New York: Random House.

Stanley, A. (1999). *Visioneering*. Sisters, Oregon: Multnomah Publishers.

Stark, R. (1997). *The Rise of Christianity*. Princeton: Harper Collins.

The American Society for Aesthetic Plastic Surgery. (n.d.). *2008 Statistics*. Retrieved 06 18, 2009, from The American Society for Aesthetic Plastic Surgery: http://www.surgery.org/download/2008stats.pdf

The Barna Group. (2003). *Stewardship*. Retrieved 12 12, 2008, from The Barna Group: http://www.barna.org/FlexPage.aspx?Page=Topic&TopicID=36

The Miracle. (2008). Retrieved 06 21, 2009, from Cave Church: http://www.cavechurch.com/miracle/index.asp

Tomlin, C., Walt, J., & Reeves, J. (Composers). (2001). The Wonderful Cross. [C. Tomlin, Performer] On *The Noise We Make*. Six Step Records.

UNHCR. (2005). *2005 UNHCR Statistical Yearbook*. Retrieved 04 09, 2009, from United Nations High Commission for Refugees: http://www.unhcr.org/statistics/STATISTICS/4641835bb.pdf

UNICEF. (2008). *State of the World Children 2008*. Retrieved 12 11, 2008, from UNICEF: http://www.unicef.org/sowc08/

UNICEF. (1995). *State of the Worlds Children*. New York: Oxford University Press.

United Nations Development Program. (2006). *Human Development Report 2006*. New York: Palgrave Macmillan.

United Nations. (n.d.). *End Poverty Millennium Development Goals 2015*. Retrieved 11 29, 2009, from United Nations: http://www.un.org/millenniumgoals/

United Nations. (2007). *The Millennium Development Goals Report*. Retrieved 12 11, 2008, from United Nations: http://www.un.org/millenniumgoals/pdf/mdg2007.pdf

Viola, F. (2008). *Reimagining Church*. Nashville: David C. Cook.

World Bank Development Indicators 2008. (2008, 04). *Poverty Facts and Stats*. Retrieved 12 11, 2008, from Global Issues: http://www.globalissues.org/article/26/poverty-facts-and-stats#src16

World Health Organization. (n.d.). *Health in Water Resources Development*. Retrieved September 4, 2009, from World Health Organization: http://www.who.int/docstore/water_sanitation_health/vector/water_resources.htm

World Health Organization. (2008). *Safe Water, Better Health*. Spain: World Health Organization Press.

Wuthnow, R. (2009). *Boundless Faith: The Global Outreach of American Churches*. Los Angeles: University of California Press.

Yancey, P. (2006). *Prayer*. Grand Rapids: Zondervan.

End Notes

Introduction: Status Quo is Not an Option

1   Stanley, *Visioneering,* 1999, p. 17

2   Berry Sr. & Reynolds, *Reflections On My Life: Louis Pasteur*

3   Blanchard & Hodges, *The Servant Leader,* 2003, pp. 45-46

4   Sharma, *Leadership Wisdom from The Monk Who Sold His Ferrari: The 8 Rituals of Visionary Leaders,* 1998, p. 48

5   Ibid, pp. 56-57

6   Hybels, *Holy Discontent,* 2007, p. 27

7   Sider R. J., *Rich Christians in an Age of Hunger,* 1997, p. 3

8   Yancey, *Prayer,* 2006, p. 105

Chapter 1 How Badly We're Broken

1   NASA, *NASA Budget Information,* 2009

2   Food and Agriculture Organization of the United Nations, *The State of Food Insecurity In The World,* 2005

3   Sider R. J., *Rich Christians in an Age of Hunger,* 1997, p. 10

Chapter 2 The Picture of Their Physical Poverty

1   Ravallion, Chen, & Sangraula, *Dollar A Day Revisited*, 2008, p. 3

2   Ibid, p. 23

3   Chen & Ravallion, *The Developing World Is Poorer Than We Thought*, 2008, p. 19

4   *2005 World Population Data Sheet*, 2005

5   Chen & Ravallion, *The Developing World Is Poorer Than We Thought*, 2008, p. 32

6   Bourke, *The Skeptic's Guide to Global Poverty*, 2007, p. 45

7   Ibid, p. 21

8   Ibid, p. 27

9   United Nations, *The Millennium Development Goals Report*, 2007, p. 11

10   World Bank Development Indicators, *Poverty Facts and Stats*, 2008

11   Ibid

12   Global Issues, *Global Issues*, 2008

13   UNICEF, *State of the World Children 2008*, 2008, p. 42

14   Bourke, *The Skeptic's Guide to Global Poverty*, 2007, p. 53

15   Ibid, p. 55

16   United Nations Development Program, *Human Development Report 2006*, 2006, p. 45

17   World Health Organization, *Safe Water, Better Health*, 2008

18 World Health Organization, *Health in Water Resources Development*

19 UNICEF, *State of the Worlds Children*, 1995, p. 59

20 Global Issues, *Global Issues*, 2008

21 Sharp, *U.S. Defense Spending, 2001-2009*, 2008

22 National Defence, *Defence Budgets 1999-2007*, 2008

23 Sider R. J., *Rich Christians in an Age of Hunger*, 1997, p. 17

24 Business Week, *Diet Industry*, 2008

25 The American Society for Aesthetic Plastic Surgery, *2008 Statistics*, p. 16

26 Sider R. J., *Rich Christians in an Age of Hunger*, 1997, p. 23

27 Ropelato, *Internet Pornography Statistics*, 2006

28 Global Issues, *Global Issues*, 2008

29 Ibid

30 *Cellular News*, 2006

31 Ibid

32 Global Issues, *Global Issues*, 2008

33 Ibid

34 Ibid

35 Viola, *Reimagining Church*, 2008, p. 89

36 Ibid

37 Jacquet, *Yearbook of American and Canadian Churches*, 1991, p. 305

38 Gordon-Conwell Theological Seminary, *Status of Global Mission 2008*, 2007

39   Ibid

40   Ibid

41   Ronsvalle & Ronsvalle, *The State of Church Giving through 2004*, 2006, p. 53

42   Organization for Economic Cooperation and Development, 2005

43   Global Issues, *Global Issues*, 2008

44   Singer, *The Life You Can Save, 2009, p. 3*

45   Ibid, p. 39

Chapter 3 The Picture of Our Spiritual Poverty

1   Ronsvalle & Ronsvalle, *The State of Church Giving through 2004*, 2006, p. 36

2   The Barna Group, *Stewardship*, 2003

3   Ibid

4   Bibby, *Religion in the Twenty-First Century: The Canadian Case*, 1986, p. 3

5   Evangelical Fellowship of Canada, *What are Canadians Saying to the Church*, 2004

6   The Barna Group, *Stewardship, 2003*

7   Gallup International, *Millennium Survey*, 2000

8   Sider R. J., *The Scandal of the Evangelical Conscience*, 2005, pp. 27-28

Chapter 4 Christians Are Just a Bunch of Hypocrites

1   Kinnaman, *unChristian*, 2007, p. 48

2   Ibid, p. 50

3   Ibid, p. 27

4   Koszarycz, *Constantinian Christianity*, 1999

5   Constantine I and Christianity, 2009

6   Aristides, *In The Meantime*, 2009

7   Stark, *The Rise of Christianity*, 1997, pp. 5-7

8   Ibid, pp. 74-75

9   Cavey, *The End of Religion*, 2005, p. 36

10 Kinnaman, *unChristian*, 2007, p. 40

Chapter 5 The Old Testament Picture

1   Malick, *An Introduction to the Book of Ezekiel*, p. 8

2   Graves, *Amos*, 2000

3   Gallagher, *The True Cost of Low Prices*, 2006, pp. 75, 77

4   Graves, *Amos*, 2000

Chapter 6 The New Testament Picture

1   Maher, http://www.youtube.com/watch?v=PHH2JItePlc, 2008

2   Ibid

3   McLaren, *The Secret Message of Jesus: Uncovering The Truth That Could Change Everything*, 2006, p. 31

4   Barna, *Revolution*, 2005, p. 25

5   UNHCR, *2005 UNHCR Statistical Yearbook*, 2005

6   Blue Letter Bible, http://www.blueletterbible.org/Bible.cf
m?b=Jam&c=1&v=26&t=NLT#conc/27

7   Blomberg, *Neither Poverty Nor Riches*, 1999, p. 160

8   Ibid, pp. 178-179

Chapter 7 Change

1   Barna, *Revolution*, 2005, pp. 13-14

Chapter 8 The Holy Spirit, Prayer, and Worship

1   *Effects of Revival*, http://www.welshrevival.com/

2   *History of the Mendicant Friars*, http://www.historyworld.
net/wrldhis/PlainTextHistories.asp?HistoryID=aa90&Para
graphID=gfq#gfq

3   *History Of The Jesuits*, http://www.historyworld.net/
wrldhis/PlainTextHistories.asp?historyid=ab30

4   Edwards, *Jonathan Edwards: On the Great Awakening*,
1743

5   Barna, *Revolution*, 2005, pp. 103, 105

Chapter 9 Self-Centered Living vs. Self-Emptying Love

1   Piper, *A Hunger For God*, 1997, p. 11

2   Tomlin, Walt, & Reeves, *The Noise We Make*, 2001

3   McManus, *An Unstoppable Force*, 2001, pp. 23, 33

4   Sider R. J., *Rich Christians in an Age of Hunger*, 1997, p. 17

5   Business Week, *Diet Industry*, 2008

6   Ropelato, *Internet Pornography Statistics*, 2006

7   Global Issues, *Global Issues*, 2008

8   Ibid

9   Ibid

10   Ibid

11   Viola, *Reimagining Church*, 2008, p. 89

12   Ibid

13   Millennium Project, 2005

14   Singer, *The Life You Can Save*, 2009, p. 143

15   Ibid, p. 152

16   Rowell, *To Give or Not To Give?*, 2006, pp. 9-10

17   Sider R. J., *Rich Christians in an Age of Hunger*, 1997, p. 22

18   Sachs, *The End Of Poverty*, 2005, pp. 232-235

19   Sider R. J., *Rich Christians in an Age of Hunger*, 1997, p. 39

Chapter 10 The First Steps of Leadership

1   Sider R., *Are Evangelical Leaders On Their Way To Hell?*, 2001

Chapter 11 The Scary Transformational Power of Total Dependence

1   *The Miracle*, 2008

Chapter 12 A Captivating Vision of a Preferred Future

1   Wuthnow, *Boundless Faith: The Global Outreach of American Churches*, 2009, p. 7

2   Ibid, p. 6

LaVergne, TN USA
13 December 2010
208581LV00004B/59/P